The Mystery of the Portland Vase

The Mystery of the Portland Vase

Robin Brooks

Duckworth

First published in 2004 by
Gerald Duckworth and Co. Ltd
90-93 Cowcross Street
London EC1M 6BF
Tel. 020 7490 7300
Fax 020 7490 0080
inquiries@duckworth-publishers.co.uk
www.ducknet.co.uk

A CIP catalogue record for this book is available
from the British Library

ISBN 0 7156 3211 6

Typeset by Ray Davies
Printed and bound in Great Britain by
Creative Print and Design, Wales

Table of Fragments

Acknowledgements

Thanks to the British Museum, for permission to use the images of the Vase, and in particular to Dr. Susan Walker, Deputy Curator of the Department of Greek and Roman Antiquities. Of all the sources used, a special debt of gratitude is owed to the experts who compiled the Journal of Glass Studies, Vol. 32, the most thorough and scholarly account of the Vase in all its aspects: William Gudenrath, Kenneth Painter, David Whitehouse, and Ian C. Freestone. Thanks also to Eleanor Birne at Duckworth, Simon Trewin and Claire Scott at PFD, Alix Bunyan-Hawley for patient copy-editing, to my wife Fiona McAlpine for all her encouragement and support, and last and least to Clive Brill.

List of Illustrations

Plates: © Copyright The British Museum.

Prologue

Go up the main steps of the British Museum and into the foyer (entrance is free). Resist the flow of visitors drawn forwards by the magnificent vista of the new Great Court straight ahead; on the left-hand side of the foyer is a broad stairway leading up, and you must steer towards it, through the swirl of tourists and schoolchildren. It has a slightly neglected air; once the main stairway, it has been sidelined by the radical alterations to the central courtyard of the Museum, and there is something dim and grey and shabby about it. Go up it all the same, up two wide, high, echoing flights, and you will arrive on the upper floor of the Museum. Turn sharp right, and start to walk through the galleries. This route will take you through a Bronze Age gallery, the HSBC Money Gallery, and finally down the long straight run of Galleries 69 to 73, devoted to Ancient Greece and Rome. There are many treasures here, and about halfway down you will find the Portland Vase, the most famous of them all, sitting on a plinth, at about chest height.

It's easy to walk straight past, even if you are looking for it. It's small, squat even, barely taller than the span of your hand: nine and three-quarter inches high, and only seven inches across at its widest point. There's a significant chance that it will be obscured from view by a small group of tourists; the Vase is a highlight on tours of the

Museum, and as like as not a guide will be holding forth about it, though very possibly in a language you cannot understand. Wait until they have moved on, or elbow your way through, and take a closer look.

Once you see the Vase properly, you realise that after all there is something striking about it. For one thing, it is different from everything else in the gallery. All around are stone and terracotta and other imperishable materials. There are many objects of metal: bronze, silver, even gold. But nothing like the Vase, because the Vase is made of glass: cobalt blue, blue-black glass, opaque, with a deep, dull sheen. It has an air about it. It is so fragile, delicate, and yet so *old* – as much as two thousand years old. What has it seen? By whom has it been handled and admired in that time? Who sold it or gave it? Who borrowed or bought it?

A decorative frieze runs around the body of the Vase. It is an outer skin of white glass that has been carved away, leaving figures in relief, and where the white glass has been removed the blue remains as the backdrop to the scene. The carving is extraordinarily delicate; some parts of the white glass have been carved down to a thinness that allows the blue to show through underneath, providing effects of shading, shadow and distance. Two handles of blue glass connect the neck with the shoulder of the Vase. Below these runs the frieze of figures, set in a landscape of stylised trees and rocks. There are seven figures, divided into two scenes by the handles. On one side: a young man, with a cloak hanging from his hand; a young woman, seated, with a serpent between her thighs, who reaches out behind her to clasp the young man's outstretched arm; a cupid flies above them with a bow and torch; a bearded man, standing with his hand to his chin. On the other side: a young man, seated on rocks; a young woman, lying on a rocky bed, with a torch upended in her loosened fingers; a woman seated, holding a long staff.

There is another object beside the Vase: a disc of blue, again overlaid with white, carved glass. This disc once served as the base of the Vase. The carving shows the head and shoulders of a man, wearing a soft 'Phrygian' cap. He is holding his finger to his lips, as though doubtful, or keeping a secret.

Who are these figures? Who carved them and what were they meant to signify? The Vase is silent. Here it sits, frozen, seemingly immortal, and pregnant with secrets. But look more closely still, and you will see that the surface of the Vase is webbed with fine cracks; it has suffered during its long life. Here is palpable evidence of some catastrophic event – a first clue in the mystery and the extraordinary history of the Portland Vase.

First Fragment
Breaking

7 February 1845 could not be described as a quiet day at the British Museum. The Museum was halfway through a painful process of total transformation, from its original home in the outmoded and outgrown Montague House, to the large new building designed by Robert Smirke, which was going up piecemeal in its place. The Museum was a building site; Montague House was being slowly demolished and beside it the new wing, known as the Lycian Gallery, intended to hold treasures from excavations in Anatolia, was rising apace. The site was covered with labourers, great wooden beams of scaffolding, draught animals, and even soldiers to guard the works. Iron wall-ties were being forged *in situ*, a rather rickety-looking contraption called a 'traveller' conveyed massive blocks of Portland stone (no relation) about the site, and top-hatted supervisors stalked

through the confusion. The Keeper of Manuscripts, Frederic Madden, was still living with his family (including a heavily pregnant wife) in what was left of the old buildings. He complained of the 'insufferable dirt and noise'. His water supply had been cut off; rats and bugs, fleeing the demolition, infested his apartments; and the western wall of the building was leaning at an angle which left him 'in continual dread of its falling down and burying himself and his family in ruins'. The new structures were no safer than the old; a contemporary artist recorded an accident during the building of the Lycian Gallery in which a five-ton girder being hoisted up to the roof – a process which took four hours – broke loose and crashed to the ground, breaking into fragments, but mercifully missing the workmen beneath.

In all this chaos the business of the Museum went on as best it could. The Vase sat under its glass cover in Gallery Nine, and at the end of a freezing winter afternoon a handful of visitors strolled about, enjoying the last ever look at the Vase in its pristine state. A young man had entered the room, with 'something strange in his looks and manner'. He waited until the attendant had walked out into the larger, adjoining Gallery Ten, then he picked up a large fragment of sculpture from the ancient city of Persepolis that was lying to hand, and heaved it at the Vase. Had he hit it fair and square, he would have reduced the Vase to an irreparable cloud of splinters and dust, but his hand was shaky, his aim was off, and the greater part of the missile hit the floor, leaving a hefty dent in the flagstone. Nevertheless, the solid glass cover was broken through, and the Vase itself smashed into more than two hundred pieces. Something that was born under the Caesars and had survived countless generations perished in an instant.

The noise brought both the public and the attendants running, to stare at the mess. It brought 'officers of the department' from an adjoining room, and they acted with commendable speed, immediately ordering the attendants to close the doors to Galleries

Nine and Ten. The five members of the public still in Gallery Nine were asked to walk next door, where they were questioned by the Keeper of Antiquities, Mr Hawkins. Four of them, understandably worried that they might be falsely accused of complicity in the outrage, answered promptly. The fifth hung back until directly confronted. 'A stout young man, in a kind of pilot coat, with both hands in his pockets before him, replied, when questioned, in a dogged and determined tone, "I did it" '. He was handed over to a police officer. The attendants began gingerly to clear up the mess. Frederic Madden, summoned by a messenger, arrived to view what was left of the Vase, as is described in E. Miller's *That Noble Cabinet: a history of the British Museum*:

On proceeding up to the room where it was exhibited, I found it strewed on the ground in a thousand pieces, and was informed that a short time before a young man who had watched his opportunity when the room was clear, had taken up one of the large sculptured Babylonian stones, and dashed the Vase, together with the glass cover over it, to atoms! The man, apparently, is quite sane, and sober.

For Madden, no democrat, the moral was clear, and he confided it to his journal:

This is the result of exhibiting such valuable and unique specimens of art to the mob! Had the *facsimile* been shewn to them, and the *original* kept in Mr Hawkins's room, this irreparable mischief could not have taken place. Indeed as to the mob of visitors, I am so confident that they never regarded it, that if the stone which broke it, were put in its place, it would excite a great deal more attention. It is really monstrous to witness such wanton destruction! I am quite grieved about it.

Yet what will be the punishment? Perhaps a fine of a few pounds or a month's imprisonment and he may then come out and destroy something else!

A trustee of the Museum happened to be on site, looking at manuscripts in Madden's room, and it fell to him to grovel to the Duke of Portland, who had loaned his Vase to the Museum, with news of the 'most lamentable occurrence which has happened only a few minutes ago within our walls ... I have this minute come from the room, where the attendants are occupied in sweeping up the remnants of what less than an hour ago was one of the noblest ornaments of this great National Collection, and a monument of your Grace's liberality and of the trust you reposed in our safe-keeping.' The Duke replied, with remarkable understanding and forbearance, that the catastrophe was 'a misfortune against which no vigilance could have guarded it on the part of the Officers of the Museum ... I have no doubt that that man who broke the Vase whoever he is is mad ... It is perhaps fortunate that his madness has shewed itself in the way it has done instead of injury to human life.' But according to Frederic Madden, and many others who met the man, he was not mad. Who was he, and why had he done what he did? The young man had been taken before the magistrate at Bow Street for a preliminary interview, but had refused to cooperate, offering no explanation for his actions, not even giving his name. He was taken down to the cells. All that eventually could be discovered about him was that he had exactly ninepence on his person; that he had been lodging at a coffee house in Long Acre, Covent Garden, not far from the Museum; that he was living under the name of William Lloyd, but this was not his real identity; and that he was from Ireland. These details were duly recorded in the *Times* the next day, 8 February, and as the reporters had nothing else to go on, they resorted to speculation: 'It is therefore assumed that his only motive for committing the wanton destruction of this ancient and national relic was a morbid desire of notoriety, strengthened, no doubt, by straitened circumstances.'

Three days later the young man was again brought before Magistrate Mr Jardine at Bow Street for a full hearing. The landlady of the coffee house was first examined, and revealed that when the defendant had first arrived at her establishment he had given the name Lloyd and told her that he was a theatrical scene-painter just arrived from Dublin, and that he had lost his trunk. She also described him as 'regular in his habits', keeping to himself and avoiding the public rooms. There were more revelations: William had talked of how he left Dublin with a servant girl, and with eight hundred pounds in his pocket. Then he was brought in, and everyone – *Times* reporters, Museum officials and learned counsel – could have a good look at him. At the time of the outrage he had been described as 'stout', but now he seemed 'thin'. Perhaps the image he projected at the scene of the crime had been inflated by the emotional charge of his violent action, and certainly three penniless days in the cells would have been a deflating experience. He was in his early twenties, fair-haired, appeared 'delicate', and reinforced this impression by speaking in a low, weak voice and the soft southern Irish accent. Significantly, his clothes were good, and in an age when social distinctions were clearly marked by appearance this was hard evidence that he did not come from the lower orders. He was not a member of the brutish mob that Madden feared; as his speech revealed, he was educated, and from a relatively well-to-do background. Arrayed against him were Sir Henry Ellis, Chief Librarian of the Museum, Keeper of Antiquities Edward Hawkins, two solicitors to the trustees – Messrs Barnwell and Lutwidge – and the counsel for the prosecution, Mr Bodkin (a name that surely even Dickens could not have bettered). There was no counsel for the defence; the prisoner stood alone in the dock.

Proceedings were recorded in the *Times* word for word. The clerk of the court asked the accused if he still refused to give his name and address. The prisoner replied, 'Yes, Sir, I do. I wish to say that my reason for refusing to give my name is simply this – that I do not wish to involve others in the disgrace which I have brought upon myself.' Having begun, he went straight on to the root of the matter; after being left to meditate on his actions in his cell, he seemed to want to unburden himself immediately. He was now not talking just to the clerk, but to the whole court. First came a confession: 'I certainly broke the vase, and all I can say in extenuation of my conduct is, that I had been indulging in intemperance for a week before, and was then only partially recovered from the effects which that indulgence had produced upon my mind.' This was not an explanation, but the prisoner immediately tried to supply this too, apparently as best he could:

> I was suffering at the time from a kind of nervous excitement –
> a continual fear of everything I saw; and it was under this
> impression, strange as it may appear, that I committed the act
> for which I was deservedly taken into custody at the Museum. I
> can assure you, Sir, there was no *malice prepense* – no design or
> evil intention whatever on my part towards any person.

The prisoner quoted legal jargon, as though to reinforce his social status and make it clear he was no mere yahoo. Was he, or had he been, a law student? What of his explanation? Psychoanalysis and psychiatry were hardly even in their infancy – Freud was born more than a decade after the smashing of the Vase – but now the twenty-first-century reader reaches automatically for diagnoses such as 'nervous breakdown', 'paranoia' and 'schizophrenia'. Even for us, armed with modern knowledge, the proffered explanation still leaves much in obscurity. Had some sort of mental disturbance driven him to flee from Dublin, or had he just eloped with the servant girl? Was some problem in his relationship with this girl the cause of his outburst? There was no sign of her now in court, or anywhere else. Were the eight hundred pounds a fiction, or an exaggeration, or had he really acquired this money in some way and run through it all? Had the girl abandoned him when the cash ran out? Most importantly, what drove him into Gallery Nine that wintry afternoon? Did he just come in to escape the cold, or had he been haunting the gallery for days, peering continually at the Vase, and deliberately singling it out for destruction? If he, as the *Times* had suggested, harboured a 'morbid desire of notoriety', why then was he refusing to reveal his true identity? He had told his landlady he was a 'scene-painter'; was this just a cover, to explain his presence in Drury Lane, the centre of the London theatre world, or did he really have some artistic training, that might have led him, out of obsession or envy, to the Vase?

It is difficult to prevent the imagination from providing answers to these questions. Inexplicable acts of violence are the currency of modern novelists, and one can picture 'William Lloyd' as a dysfunctional protagonist, like Raskolnikov or Stephen Dedalus, with the blank city streets, the cheap room, and the disconnected thoughts of stifling mother or tearful girlfriend grinding round and round. But the temptation must be resisted, because none of these questions can now be answered; they make up still more mysteries to add to those surrounding the Vase.

In any case, explanations did not concern Mr Bodkin, who was merely out for justice, and revenge. But – unable to live up to his name – he could not at first get to the point. He was a Member of Parliament, and not the sort of lawyer to use one word where twenty would do. He expatiated on the 'beautiful and valuable specimen of art which the prisoner had wantonly destroyed whilst exercising that privilege which was open to the public without restriction'. He described how the medical officers had found the prisoner to be of sound mind, and therefore responsible for his actions. He took for granted the prisoner's guilt, and the rest of his speech was concerned not with whether but with how the prisoner should be punished. Here he acknowledged an unfortunate aspect of the law – something, even, of a loophole. The only way the offence could be dealt with was under section twenty-four of the Wilful Damage Act. He read the relevant sections of tortuous legal language to the court. He debated their interpretation at length, having detected an ambiguity. Any person guilty of damage 'shall forfeit or pay such sum of money as shall appear to the justice to be a reasonable compensation for the damage, injury, or spoil so committed, not exceeding the sum of five pounds'. Did this sum refer to the value of the object damaged, or the amount of the fine? If the former, then it would appear that the prisoner would escape punishment, for there was no getting over the fact that the Vase was worth rather more. This vandal would get off scot-free, in other words. Bodkin himself did not welcome this conclusion. He warned the magistrate of the consequences: open season would be declared on the treasures of the British Museum; any member of the public would be able to wander in and smash whatever he chose with impunity. He quoted the precedent of the man who had thrust his walking-stick into a painting in the National Gallery, and who had been successfully fined by Magistrate Maltby at Marlborough Street under section twenty-four, despite the potential loophole. He sat down.

The magistrate, who had doubtless been frowning through all this, turned first to the prisoner: 'You have heard the statements which have been made to the Court. I am now prepared to hear anything further that you may wish to say.' The prisoner thought it best to abase himself: 'Whatever be the punishment you may feel it your duty to award me, I shall have the consolation of feeling that it has been richly deserved.' But Mr Jardine had not made up his mind. He baulked at the loophole and could not simply follow Mr Maltby. 'It seems to me very doubtful whether I have any power at all to act in the charge before me, and therefore I shall take time to give that question more consideration,' he said.

One can imagine Bodkin sighing before rising to his feet again. Fortunately, he had a cunningly prepared fallback position: in addition to the complete demolition of the Portland Vase, a glazed case, by which it was covered, and which belonged to the trustees of the Museum, was also destroyed. The value of this case was less than five pounds, and therefore, without reference to the Vase, he was instructed to proceed against the prisoner for the damage caused to the less important article. So, thanks to the complexities of the law, the prisoner was convicted of the destruction not of the Vase, but of the case in which it sat. Mr Jardine was now ready to pass sentence: 'There could be no doubt that, in the eye of the law, the prisoner had been guilty of wilfully and maliciously destroying this property, and –'

But at this point the prisoner made his only protest, interrupting the magistrate: 'It was not maliciously done,' he objected. Mr Jardine answered, 'The law attributes malice to all such acts as these, in the absence of any other causes to which they could be ascribed … I therefore convict you of the offence, and order you to pay three pounds; in default of which I commit you to hard labour in the House of Correction for two months.' The prisoner was removed.

He was sent to Tothill Fields prison, where he immediately got on the wrong side of the turnkey, and was handcuffed and put in solitary confinement. Perhaps this was because he was too much a gentleman; in the early Victorian period London's criminal underclass was often excessively brutal and base, and a well-dressed student, however impecunious, might have been singled out. Wolf Mankowitz, in a book about the Wedgwood copies of the Vase, suggests that 'Lloyd may have harboured other and even darker impulses, for which he was glad to gain correction', and that, disappointed with the leniency of his sentence, he took steps to exacerbate his punishment. But if so, he was frustrated. Only two days later a crudely written letter arrived for Mr Jardine. It read, 'I take the liberty of enclosing three pounds as wich is the paultry penalty in default of paying wich you have sentenced my relation through Adam and Eve poor Mister William Lloyd the Irish gintleman to two months hard labour.' Three freshly minted gold sovereigns accompanied the letter, together with a warning that a copy had gone to the prisoner, so that the letter could not be ignored. Who had done this, and why? The mysterious benefactor supplied only a joke against the legal profession by way of explanation – he was himself, he said, 'an Irish Attorney', and having 'robbed and imprisoned so many', paying for the prisoner's release would 'afford his consence some rest'.

The prisoner was released, but the trustees of the Museum were not done with him. They put him under surveillance, and took steps to discover his true identity. 'Lloyd' had admitted to being a pupil at Trinity College, Dublin; now the college tentatively identified this pupil as one William Mulcahy, who had entered in the summer, and then disappeared. The trustees employed a private agent called Leonard Dobbin to investigate the Mulcahy family, hoping perhaps to bring a suit for damages. But Dobbin discovered that the father was dead, and 'the mother is poor ... there is no property among them'. William had a brother who had studied at Trinity and was now a private tutor. His mother was a widow, 'heartbroken' by her son's disappearance, but blissfully ignorant of the whole affair. The trustees told the Duke of Portland of their findings, but he was once again in forgiving mood: he would, he said, 'be very sorry' to make Mulcahy's family suffer for 'an act of folly or madness which they could not control'. There the matter rested, and whether William Mulcahy survived this episode, and went on to live a normal if obscure life with his servant girl, or whether he spiralled down into misery and madness, is not known.

Second Fragment
Making

Glass is a tricky thing to work with, a paradoxical substance. Apparently solid, it retains the structure and properties of a liquid. It is capable of displaying enormous strength; in theory a glass fibre can support more weight than steel. It is hard enough to blunt the sharpest, toughest cutting tools, and it is durable; it does not decay, and can survive millennia untarnished. But it is also extremely fragile and brittle. Because of its liquid structure, nothing will stop a crack from spreading once one starts. Although strong in compression it is weak in tension. It is a poor conductor of heat, and a sudden change in temperature will create internal stresses that may prove fatal. If glass heats up, its surface will come under the force of compression as it rises in temperature before the glass underneath it. If the glass is cooling, then the surface is put under tension, and this makes it even more vulnerable.

Glass occurs naturally, in the form of obsidian, a black glass created by certain types of cooling lava, but people began to manufacture it at a very early date. Glass has been excavated from sites five thousand years old, and glass vessels have been discovered in Egyptian tombs. Tablets from the Royal Library of King Ashurbanipal at Nineveh, written some time in the seventh century BC, carry recipes for the making of glass. The Roman writer Pliny tells a story of how glass was invented: a group of merchants, camping on the banks of a river, decided to use the blocks of soda they were carrying as supports for their cooking pots. In the morning they discovered that the heat from the cooking fires had turned the sand and soda into a miraculous new material. This story, however, is apocryphal; temperatures of more than a thousand degrees centigrade are needed to make the necessary ingredients fuse, far higher than could be generated by a cooking fire at a bivouac.

Early glass was coloured by the addition of iron oxides and used to imitate precious stones; the treasures of Tutankhamun are much decorated with such productions. Blue was the favourite colour of glass-makers, created by the addition of tiny amounts of cobalt and copper. White glass was made by adding antimony, which could also be used to produce clear glass. The first glass vessels were made by covering a core of straw and mud on a metal rod with molten glass. When the glass had cooled, this core could be picked out. Then vessels were built up from rods of molten glass, bent into circles and fused together to build what is known as mosaic glass.

The technique of glass-blowing was developed in Roman times, and the basic process has not much changed in the last two thousand years. Some time in the first century BC, glass-workers discovered that a gob of molten glass, set onto the end of a hollow metal rod, could be inflated into a globe, and then shaped into a vessel. At first they blew the molten glass into prepared moulds to give the desired shape, but they soon discovered they could dispense with these. The technique was perfected, possibly by Syrian craftsmen, and spread quickly across the Roman Empire. Right from the start it was recognised that there was something special about the manufacture of glass, an alchemical mystique which put it above other trades. Glass-makers kept their trade secrets closely guarded, and they had cachet. A street was named after them in Ancient Rome. In the later Empire they were exempt from taxation. By the time of the Renaissance they were a class apart, and even regarded as on a par with the aristocracy.

Blown glass was a luxury in Ancient Roman times. The emperor Nero paid huge sums for blown glass cups, and is even said to have regarded broken fragments of rare vessels as worth keeping. His friend and adviser Petronius wrote a novel which satirises the crass ostentation of a nouveau-riche called Trimalchio. This oafish nabob boasts of his glassware, rating it above even his Corinthian bronze dinner-set because it 'doesn't smell'. If it wasn't so fragile, he declares, he would prefer it to gold. Trimalchio then tells the story of a craftsman who discovers the secret of unbreakable glass, which he demonstrates to the emperor by dropping a piece of it on the pavement. He then picks up his work, and casually hammers out the slight resulting dent. The emperor, impressed, asks if he has shared his secret with anyone else, and when the man replies in the negative, has him taken out and beheaded, in order to protect Roman industry. This little joke shows how glass was still regarded as something new and remarkable in Imperial times.

Cameo glass was also developed by the Romans. Cameos were sculptures carved in low relief on precious stones. Craftsmen took advantage of the naturally occurring layers of different colour in a precious stone like agate or onyx to create a work in which the carving stood out from the layer beneath. A taste for such items was supposed to have been developed by the Romans after they defeated Mithridates, King of Pontus, and looted his treasures, among which were many cameo gems. The historian Pliny lamented the deleterious effect this influx of outside tastes had on the simple values that had made the Republic great, and turned up his Roman nose at the kitsch extravagance of the warlord Pompey, who at his triumph over Mithridates paraded a portrait of himself made entirely of pearls. But neither Pliny nor anyone else could hold back the tide of imported luxuries, as Republican Rome exercised its growing military might by conquering the decadent Hellenistic empires and plundering their treasure-houses. Artists and craftsmen gravitated to the new centre of power and patronage to cater for the tastes of the new rulers, and with them came glass-makers and engravers from Syria and Alexandria. The Roman elite now acquired the tastes of the conquered, and the wealth to satisfy them. Any Roman with pretensions to rank had to have his own carved seal. Both cameos and intaglio work (in which the design is cut into the surface) were popular. The dictator Sulla collected carved gemstones, and Julius Caesar himself developed a passion for them.

Very early on, glass-makers learned to imitate the naturally occurring layers of colour in gemstones, and thus produce items which would satisfy the growing demand. Instead of adapting a design to the haphazard layers of an appropriately formed, naturally occurring stone, the engravers could dictate the form and colour of layers of glass, and could then go confidently to work, secure in the knowledge that no natural irregularity was going to spoil their efforts. Glass 'gems' and plaques, which could be carved into cameos, were produced by craftsmen who directly transferred their skills from the cutting of gemstones. Some stones, like agate, sardonyx and chalcedony, are softer than glass, but some, like quartz and obsidian, are harder. The engraver, or *diatretarius*, had already perfected his skills of cutting, carving and polishing, and simple lathes had been developed, grinding wheels that could be fed with abrasives, to supplement the hand-tools. So great was the engravers' skill that microscopes are now needed to appreciate the complexities of some cameo carving. The craftsmen themselves, of course, did not have magnifying lenses of any kind, and how they managed to carve these details remains a mystery; it has been suggested that myopic individuals were employed, in order to take advantage of their naturally close vision.

With the development of blown glass, the cameo technique was extended to vessels. The Roman glass-makers had discovered the secret of creating works made up of layers of different glass. These are extremely difficult to produce, because different kinds of glass will contract at different rates, and if an item is made up of these, potentially fatal tensions are created as it cools, which can cause a work to fly apart at the touch of a fingernail, or merely at a change in the ambient temperature. But these problems were overcome. A blown glass vessel, while still hot, was dipped into, or overlaid with, another layer of glass, blown, shaped and then cooled slowly in an oven by a process known as annealing. The overlay could then be carved away to create a cameo vessel. Such works represent the highest achievement of Roman craftsmanship, and the Portland Vase is the finest existing example of these, a pinnacle of the glass-maker's art.

*

William Mulcahy's lump of basalt lands on the Vase, and it explodes into fragments. These litter the floor, mixed with the ruins of the glass case under which the Vase sat. Anxious attendants clear the room, and the staff, appalled, survey the devastation. Then they get down on hands and knees, and begin to pick up the pieces. An unpleasant task: the shards are sharp enough to draw blood, and they must be careful not to kneel on them, not only for the sake of their own skin, but to avoid further damage to the remains. Some fragments are large, suggesting the possibility of restoration, but many more are splinters, anonymous, impossibly small, enough to dash the hopes of the most optimistic restorer. Bit by bit they are collected up. A few are lost for ever; the Vase will never be completely whole again. Some are difficult to identify. Perhaps they will never find their rightful place in the restoration; there will be gaps, holes, places where two pieces do not fit as they should. This complicated and frustrating process provides an obvious metaphor for the long history of the Vase. There are gaps in the sequence of events, and some of them now seem impossible to fill. There are places where the story doesn't quite make sense, however the evidence is configured and reconfigured. There are some larger pieces of the jigsaw, as the records supply generous details of a particular stage in the Vase's life and adventures, but then the records fall silent again, and only hints are left, and more lacunae appear. One of the biggest gaps is at the very beginning of the story: how does the Vase emerge into the historical record? The answer to this question is far from clear; the first mystery in the history of the Portland Vase surrounds its discovery.

Third Fragment

Discovery

In 1582 Fabrizio Lazzaro starts to dig a hole. He owns a large mound on the southern outskirts of Rome, just a few miles from the gates of the city. The mound is popularly known as the Monte del Grano, so called because it resembles a cone-shaped heap of grain. There is even a local legend that explains how impious farmers, having harvested on a holy day, saw the fruit of their labours blasted by a thunderbolt of divine outrage, and turned into this solid heap of earth. Once it was lined with marble blocks, but these have long since been carted off and burnt for their lime. A passage at ground level leads to a large, empty chamber, now robbed of its stone cladding and anything it once possessed. Monte del Grano is in fact a burial mound from the days of Imperial Rome. Lazzaro is a man of substance, with a palazzo in the city which already houses a collection of antiquities. He has a theory that above the empty tomb is hidden another, secret chamber. Hoping to prove his theory, and add to his collection, Lazzaro starts on top of the mound, and digs downwards towards the centre. He is digging for treasure.

In Rome at this time the dead appeared to outnumber the living. The sixteenth-century city huddled inside the ancient walls, leaving large tracts of wilderness. Montaigne visited the city a year before Lazzaro began to dig, and declared that nothing remained but desolation. The Forum was a cattle-market, the Arch of Constantine was up to its knees in shops and shacks, and many other monuments were buried in weeds and oblivion. The sixteenth-century Romans lived cheek-by-jowl with their past, and were contemptuously familiar with it; it was all around them, only just under their feet, and if they dug down, they would find it easily enough. They hacked up ancient foundations for building materials, and very often they found evidence of past glories – coins, statues, inscriptions. An office called *il Cavatori* evolved, a position responsible for the exploitation of whatever resources might lie below ground. An official appointed by the Pope in 1573 was the 'Commissioner of Treasures and other Antiquities, and of Mines'; the past was there to be exploited like a seam of coal.

Lazzaro digs down, through a great mass of concrete. The tumulus is getting on for fifty metres in diameter; it's a massive monument, with plenty of room for a hidden chamber, perhaps the resting place of significant remains, and who knows what might be preserved with them in the silent darkness? Lazzaro hopes to find something, but what? At the bottom of the shaft, the workman hefts his pickaxe, swings, and feels no resistance. A hole gapes black, earth trickles in; he has broken through.

The very idea of a past buried under the earth had been for some, in earlier centuries, a concept hard to grasp. Some years before Lazzaro began to dig, a Polish duke decided to excavate a field. He found many vases – funeral urns perhaps – but he could not believe that they were the work of men from past ages, surviving in the ground. He decided that they were naturally occurring phenomena; the pot-shape was just an extraordinary coincidence. These curious finds, he speculated, must have grown in the earth like seeds or tubers, and he was so taken by this theory that he adjusted the facts to fit it: when the pots first come out of the ground, he declared, they were soft and pliable, and only hardened when exposed to the daylight.

The Romans of the sixteenth century had a better understanding, but they were not all antiquarians by any means. Pope Sixtus V was busy refurbishing the city, but his efforts were directed towards the Christian monuments, the churches and catacombs. The generals and emperors of Imperial Rome were deposed from their obelisks and columns, and replaced by the statues of saints. Sixtus decided to demolish one of the great monuments of the Republic, the tomb of Cecilia Metella on the Appian Way. He wanted it for the stone, and had to be dissuaded from this act of vandalism by the protests of his more enlightened citizens. He successfully presided over the destruction of another important tomb, which stood near to the Monte del Grano. He even dreamed up a scheme to turn the Colosseum into a wool-weaving factory. Workmen had already begun to take the structure apart when, luckily for the future tourist industry and the décor of Italian restaurants worldwide, Sixtus died. But many admired classical artworks for their power of expression, for the passions they exposed and proclaimed, which were forbidden in contemporary art. The austere Pope Pius V had disbanded the collection of classical statues he inherited, seeing them as one more element of corruption to be rooted out along with the courtesans and sodomites who infected his holy city, and against whom he campaigned furiously. But not even he could bring himself to get rid of the finest works. Instead he erected wooden shutters around them and simply forbade anyone to look at them.

Lazzaro has broken into the roof of a cavern. He ropes himself up, lights a lantern, and is lowered slowly into the darkness. The swinging lantern reveals a burial chamber; below him lies a sarcophagus, and it appears to be undisturbed. Lazzaro finally stands on the floor of the chamber, disturbing the dust of centuries, perhaps the first person to have stood here since grieving relatives closed up the tomb more than a thousand years before. He examines the sarcophagus by the light of the lantern. It is a sumptuous piece of work, decorated with reliefs that show scenes from the life of Achilles – it's pre-Christian, very old. On the lid are represented two reclining figures; are these the people whose remains lie inside? Could they be members of the imperial family?

Trembling with excitement, Lazzaro orders the lifting of the heavy sarcophagus lid. What does he hope to see: the gleam of gold, the glint of gems? The chamber itself seems to be holding its breath. What he finds surpasses his expectations. Inside the sarcophagus lies one of the greatest treasures of the ancient world, priceless, unique. Lazzaro has hit the jackpot. He has found the Vase.

This account of the discovery of the Vase comes from Pietro Santo Bartoli, a seventeenth-century antiquarian, in a work on Ancient Roman tombs. Bartoli claimed that the Vase contained the ashes of Emperor Alexander Severus, and identified the two figures on the lid of the sarcophagus as those of the Emperor and his mother, Julia Mammaea. Who then was this emperor, whose ashes, Bartoli suggests, found their last resting place in the Vase itself?

Alexander Severus came to power in Rome in 222 AD. At a time when the Empire was on its slow slide into bloody chaos he was something of a rarity, as a benign and successful ruler. His reputation also depends to some extent on those who came before and after him because, by contrast, they were two of the very worst of the long line of criminals and psychopaths who ruled the late Roman Empire.

Alexander's predecessor was Elagabalus. He was a member of the imperial family; in fact he was Alexander's older cousin, but his mother had retired to the eastern city of Antioch, and Elagabalus was brought up there, in eastern ways. He was devoted to the cult of the Sun, which he worshipped as a black phallic stone. He brought his stone to Rome, set it up in the temple, and then, according to Edward Gibbon, in his *Decline and Fall of the Roman Empire*, 'corrupted by his youth, his country, and his fortune, abandoned himself to the grossest pleasures with ungoverned fury'. Gibbon is disappointingly short on detail, but he does describe 'a long train of concubines', mentions the ravishing of vestal virgins, and tells how 'the master of the Roman world affected to copy the dress and manners of the female sex'. But his conclusion is fairly explicit: 'It may seem probable, that the vices and follies of Elagabalus have been adorned by fancy. Yet attested by grave and contemporary historians, their inexpressible infamy surpasses that of any other age or country.'

Not, in other words, a particularly hard act to follow. So when the legions – who could make or break an emperor at this time – tired of Elagabalus's excesses, murdered him, threw his mutilated body into the river Tiber, and hoisted his young cousin onto the throne, Alexander Severus was already in their eyes a paragon. And he does seem to have been the very opposite of his predecessor: 'A natural mildness and moderation of temper preserved him from the assaults of passion, and the allurements of vice.' Instead of indulging in orgies and outrages, Alexander conducted himself like a philosopher-king: 'The greatest part of his morning hours was employed in his council. The dryness of business was relieved by the charms of literature. The exercises of the body succeeded to those of the mind ... Refreshed by the use of the bath and a slight dinner, he resumed, with new vigour, the business of the day.'

Peace and prosperity seemed to be returning, until, that is, Alexander and his mother — who ruled with him as regent — attempted to reform the army. A military commander called Maximinus took advantage of the disaffection this caused to stage a coup. Maximinus was 'a young barbarian of gigantic stature'. He had come up through the ranks to become the Tribune of the Fourth Legion. Cunning and ambitious, he was also in the eyes of his men a 'real soldier', and they happily murdered Alexander for his sake. He was the first emperor unable to read or write, and he seems to have nursed a massive inferiority complex, or, as Gibbon puts it, 'He was conscious that his mean and barbarian origin, his savage appearance, and his total ignorance of the arts and institutions of civil life, formed a very unfavourable contrast with the amiable manners of the unhappy Alexander.' Maximinus soon became a paranoid and murderous tyrant, somewhere between Stalin and Conan the Barbarian. Flanked by two monsters, Alexander's reputation gained by contrast until, by the time the Vase was discovered, he was regarded as a sort of pagan saint.

The Vase's connection with Alexander Severus was first mooted by a scholar named Girolamo Teti, who wrote a description of the Vase some time before Bartoli wrote of its discovery. He was convinced that the figures on the Vase referred to the story of Alexander. Who or what do the figures on the Vase actually represent? Teti's description contains the first of these theories. There will be many, many more.

In the drawing of the Vase (see plate section), the figures are labelled from left to right, A-G. A-D sit on what we will call Side I of the Vase, E-G on Side II. The second figure, B, is Cupid. He is winged, and carries a bow and arrows. He, however, is the only figure who possesses such easily identifiable attributes; the rest are up for grabs. In Teti's interpretation, on Side I, A is Alexander the Great, assisting at the birth of Alexander Severus. B is Cupid. C is Mammaea,

Alexander Severus's mother. Mammaea gave birth to her son in a temple dedicated to Alexander the Great, and on the night of that birth she dreamt of a purple serpent, foretelling his imperial destiny; there is the serpent beside her. D is Old Father Time. On Side II, E is Youth, symbolising the shortness of Alexander's reign. F is Death, symbolising, well, his death. Finally, G is an elderly man, symbolising the decrepit Roman Empire itself.

If you are looking closely – more closely perhaps than Teti himself – you might notice that G, the 'elderly man', has full breasts, rounded hips and long hair, and is, in fact, a woman. The story of the Vase is, in one respect, the story of how scholars are willing to develop a theory on the slightest grounds, and once having developed it to assert it in the very teeth of the evidence. But if you think Teti was rather imperceptive, you must understand that some of those who came after him make him look like an antiquarian Sherlock Holmes.

So do the figures on the Vase support the theory that it contained Alexander's ashes? Not really. There are a few other flaws in this theory. We know, for instance, that Alexander Severus and his mother were murdered by the legions in far-off Germany. In an age when deposed emperors had their mutilated bodies thrown into the nearest river, it seems unlikely that his ashes would have been brought back to Rome to be interred inside a vase and a large mound. We also know that the Romans simply weren't in the habit of using glass vases to store the ashes of the dead, however delicately they may have been. And we have one more problem: *we simply cannot rely on the evidence.*

Just over three centuries after Fabrizio Lazzaro opened his tumulus, another man went digging, this time in the city records. He was an Englishman, Henry Stuart-Jones, and he revealed his findings at a meeting of the British School at Rome, held in the library, in January 1909. Stuart-Jones was a celebrity of the School, an ex-director, no less, and his meeting was attended not only by members of the British community and Italian archaeologists, but also by the British Ambassador himself, Sir James Rennell Rodd. Stuart-Jones read a paper to this distinguished gathering, illustrated by lantern slides. His talk was billed 'Miscellanea Capitolina', on various topics connected with the Capitoline Museum, but its unstated theme was Administering Lethal Put-downs to Misguided Colleagues and Setting the Record Straight.

Stuart-Jones first sharpened his sword of truth on an altar in the Museum, dedicated to Jupiter. This altar carried an inscription which meant that it had been 'assigned hitherto by archaeologists (among them Mrs Strong in her *Roman Sculpture*) to the end of the Third Century AD' (*The Athenaeum,* February 1909). That 'hitherto' alone would surely have had Mrs Strong, if present, shifting nervously in her seat. Stuart-Jones pointed out that the style of the carving on the altar 'was by no means in agreement with this hypothesis', and in fact clearly dated from an earlier time, specifically the first century AD. To Stuart-Jones the case was obvious. The altar had been re-used, and the inscription added at a later date. Leaving the unfortunate Mrs Strong squashed as though beneath the weight of the altar itself, he moved on, in the same style, to another misunderstood altar, this one dedicated to the Sun. Finally he turned his attention to the Vase.

Stuart-Jones examined the evidence as presented by Pietro Santo Bartoli, the seventeenth-century artist and antiquarian who first told the story of the discovery of the Vase: 'From his time this view gradually acquired currency, and is unhesitatingly accepted by some of the eighteenth-century writers.' Stuart-Jones, however, knew how to hesitate. He had examined the official record in the Capitoline archives, and tracked down a memorandum related to the meeting of the Communal Council on 4 May 1582. At this meeting the Council had discussed whether or not to acquire the sarcophagus from the tomb in the Monte del Grano; another memo proved that by 1590 the sarcophagus was placed in the municipal collection. The discovery of the sarcophagus was thus firmly dated to the end of the sixteenth century, but what of the Vase itself? The Council, significantly, had only discussed the sarcophagus.

Now, at the climax of his performance, Stuart-Jones delivered his *coup de grâce*. He had discovered another description of the opening of the Monte del Grano, and this was not by someone writing a century after the fact, but by a contemporary: Flaminio Vacca, architect and writer, left an account of Fabrizio's excavation. It was written in 1594, only a few years after the opening of the tomb, and more than a century before Bartoli left his account. *It contains no mention of the Vase.* All Vacca says is that a sarcophagus was discovered, and in it, some ashes. But if these ashes were contained in a glass vase of exquisite workmanship and astounding rarity, Vacca does not say. How could anyone have failed to mention such a treasure? This is surely enough to destroy any faith in Bartoli's story, and in any firm connection between the Vase and the tomb in the Monte del Grano.

Bartoli, the imputation runs, made it all up in order to enhance the reputation and value of the Vase, by putting about the story that it contained the ashes of a saintly emperor. Can we blame him for this embroidery? The business about the swinging lantern and Lazzaro trembling with excitement is not in the record either. How do we know whether he was trembling or not? Maybe Lazzaro had just had a passionate altercation with his mistress and, full of rage and despair, was distracting himself with some amateur archaeology towards the outcome of which he was completely indifferent. The problem is, as a race we just can't resist telling stories, and the whole history of the Vase is testament to this unreliable but entertaining attribute. But if the Vase was not in the tomb then where was it? Stuart-Jones could only shrug; in default of other evidence it could only be concluded that the provenance of the Vase was 'absolutely unknown'.

Over the centuries Rome had suffered wave after wave of calamities. The city was sacked by the Goths under their King Alaric in 410 AD. The citizens were slaughtered, the streets filled with corpses, while the Goths piled their loot into wagons, 'and many a vase', as Gibbon appositely remarks, 'was shivered into fragments by the stroke of a battle-axe'. Only forty-five years later the city was sacked again, by the Vandals, whose name has since become synonymous with wanton destruction. In 472 AD Rome was sacked a third time, by soldiers under the leadership of the Gothic warlord Ricimer. In the following century the city was besieged by Goths again, and during its desperate defence by the famous Byzantine general, Belisarius, priceless statues were broken up and hurled down on the attackers. As the Western Empire was extinguished the city sank into the violence and obscurity of the Dark Ages, and its suffering did not end with its re-emergence in the Modern era. The city underwent what was perhaps its most savage treatment only a few decades before the opening of the Monte del Grano. In 1527, when Italy was serving as a battleground for the opposing powers of France and Spain, a Spanish army joined forces with a group of German mercenaries to revenge themselves on Pope Clement VII. They burst, leaderless, into the city, and for many days inflicted appalling cruelty and destruction. Churches were sacked, priests murdered, nuns raped, and two-thirds of the city laid waste.

How then did the Vase survive from Imperial times? It is hardly possible that for so many centuries it was simply gathering dust at the back of someone's wardrobe. It must have been underground and, to survive intact, deliberately buried. Mere common sense indicates that it was indeed buried in a tomb.

There is another theory which attempts to reconcile the conflicting evidence. In the 1990 *Journal of Glass Studies*, two modern scholars, Kenneth Painter and David Whitehouse, reassert the connection with Alexander Severus. They point out that the Monte del Grano was built with bricks that date from the time of that emperor, and was perhaps intended to be the resting place of his remains. They suggest a later emperor, Decius, who venerated Alexander Severus, could have brought his ashes back from Germany and installed them reverently in the tomb. They point out that even Flaminio Vacca says that ashes were found in the sarcophagus, although he does not describe any container. They mention a piece of legislation passed three years before the sarcophagus was sold to the Communal Council, specifically intended to protect ancient monuments from the 'greed' and 'lack of respect' of those who owned them. With sly, scholarly hints, the authors suggest that Lazzaro himself inspired this legislation because of his nefarious activities in the tomb-robbing line: that he found the Vase in the tomb, and secretly removed it (tipping the imperial dust back into the sarcophagus) in order to dispose of it and thus enjoy his reward without attracting public attention. A secret dig, then, and a swinging lantern, and trembling excitement, might not be so wide of the mark after all.

But the theory is far from conclusive, and the mystery still remains, to be picked over by scholars until civilisation runs out of ink. The only thing we know with any certainty, the first recorded, attested fact, is that at the end of the sixteenth century the Vase came into the collection of Cardinal Francesco Maria del Monte; so it is to the home of this intriguing cleric that we must follow it.

Fourth Fragment
Cardinal del Monte and Nicolas-Claude Fabri de Peiresc

Like the Vase, Cardinal Francesco Maria del Monte is himself now the subject of some controversy among scholars. But it is for his sexuality, and related matters, that the Cardinal is now famous, with which we will concern ourselves later. It seems that the Vase was able to attract the very best kind of owner, because Francesco was by all accounts a very interesting, agreeable and above all discerning individual. He was born in Venice, in the middle of the sixteenth century, and the painter Titian was at his baptism. His father was in the service of a princely family, the Della Rovere, and he grew up at court in Urbino. This court was already famous for its refined pleasures; it was the setting for Castiglione's *The Courtier*, that indispensable handbook for any gentleman-scholar still clinging to medieval ideals of chivalry and courtesy. Castiglione described the palace in Urbino as

> to the opinion of many men, the fairest that was to be found in all Italie; and so furnished it with all necessary implements belonging thereto, that it appeared not a Palace, but a Citie in forme of a Palace, and that not onelye with ordinary matters ... but also for sightliness; and to decke out withall, placed there a wondrous number of ancient images, of marble and metall, very excellent paintings and instruments of musicke of all sorts.

So Francesco was ideally placed to cultivate a knowledge of the arts, history and the antique, and we know that he became passionately interested in music and painting. In his early twenties he moved to Rome, and here he became a close friend and adviser to a member of the Medici, the ruling family of Florence. Cardinal Ferdinando de' Medici was the younger brother of the Grand Duke, and lived in great style in Rome. As his secretary even-handedly describes, 'he did not lack an inclination to licentiousness, but did not so abandon himself that he won disfavour.'

Francesco soon became indispensable to his powerful patron, even to the extent of helping to arrange his love affairs. But this relaxed lifestyle came to a dramatic end with the sudden death of the Grand Duke and his wife, apparently by poison. Ferdinando had to rush back to Florence and assume the title, and he took Francesco with him. So now Francesco was right-hand man to the new Grand Duke, and through his influence Francesco himself became a Cardinal, and returned to live in Rome. He took up residence in a Medici palace –

the Palazzo Madama – and he began to gather around him beautiful things of every description.

We have an appealing sketch of Francesco in a gossipy letter of the time. The writer exclaims in amazement over how well Francesco manages to live on what is – for a Cardinal – a fairly limited income. He has only fifty servants and they are well treated, his home is beautiful, and people seem to flock to him for the pleasure of his company, rather than for any political dealings. He has style, wit, charm and a thirst for life. The Palazzo Madama has a modest and austere façade. The ground plan is only ninety metres by sixty, but Francesco fills it with treasures. Eventually his collections contain sixty sculptures, medals, gems and cameos. There are tapestries and musical instruments, and, above all, works of art. Francesco acquires pictures by the superstars of the Renaissance: Michelangelo, Andrea del Sarto, Raphael, Leonardo da Vinci. He has no fewer than five Titians. And, of course, he has the Vase.

But there is one more important acquisition. In an upstairs room, in one of a row of cubicles in which sleep the fifty servants, a dark-skinned, curly-haired, rather surly young man has taken up residence. Francesco has – almost literally – picked him up off the streets. He is in his early twenties, and we know him now as Caravaggio.

When Francesco found him, Caravaggio was trying to make his own way in Rome, and he was struggling. He had no studio, no buyers, and no money; according to one account he had to paint his own face in the mirror because he couldn't afford to pay a model. Francesco's patronage meant everything: through it Caravaggio became the most famous painter in Italy, and the most powerful religious artist of his age. Moreover, Francesco's personal interests directly influenced Caravaggio's work. The artist's first painting for his new patron was 'The Musicians', which clearly reflects Francesco's love of music. But is that all it reflects?

In 'The Musicians', a group of boys, in off-the-shoulder white robes, prepare to sing and play. The central figure is tuning a lute, and he gazes out but away, his eyes seemingly full of tears, his red, sensual lips parted, as though he is in the grip of some passionate emotion. The homoerotic content of this, and many others of Caravaggio's paintings, is to some perfectly plain, but naturally the academics cannot agree. Apart from the paintings there is very little evidence of Caravaggio's homosexuality one way or the other, and so they turn their attention to the patron. *Was Francesco gay?* Suddenly the question is terribly important to such writers, and they now pick over his reputation in an attempt to prove or disprove the hypothesis. A contemporary, the Flemish writer Amayden, records that Francesco liked young men, and 'indulged his inclination openly'. This writer, however, was an acknowledged enemy of Francesco, writing after his death, who also accused him of being so mean that he had holes in his shoes, which last accusation certainly doesn't ring true. On the other side, there is a rather wistful letter from Francesco himself, remembering happy times spent in his youth with 'Artemisia and Cleopatra', who were, presumably, young ladies.

But anyway, so what? Caravaggio continued to paint for Francesco, and his next work was 'The Lute Player'. Again a beautiful, full-lipped boy in a very open shirt, plucking at the strings and turning on us a gaze of erotic melancholy. Yet what is important here is surely not specific sexual leanings. The lutanist is framed by fruit and flowers, fresh, fragile, transient. The flowers are placed in a glass vase, and the handling of the reflected light in the glass is a virtuoso performance. According to Caravaggio's biographer, Helen Langdon, the whole composition is redolent of the 'refined and aristocratic pleasures' of Francesco's palace: 'Caravaggio's pictures of these years have an exquisite quality, a sense of the beauty of precious and fragile objects.'

Caravaggio himself was a naturalist who turned deliberately against the classical tradition; when told that he should be copying ancient sculptures, his response was to grab a gypsy-girl off the street, and take her home to paint. That, he said, was the only fit subject: his master was nature. So he was hardly the man to be influenced by the Vase. But something of its precious nature, of its fragility, appears in his work, mediated through the exquisite taste of Cardinal Francesco del Monte.

*

We only know that the Vase belonged to del Monte because of the writings of a Frenchman, Nicolas-Claude Fabri de Peiresc. De Peiresc in fact supplies us with our first official sighting of the Vase, long before Girolamo Teti recounted his story of the finding of the Vase in the Monte del Grano. This is entirely appropriate and pleasing, because de Peiresc is regarded by many as the first real antiquarian. Those who play the major parts in the story of the Vase divide roughly into two groups: the rich and powerful who owned the Vase, and the learned, who studied it. Rarely, an individual manages to straddle both categories, but more often we will find ourselves alternating between the two. Cardinal del Monte was one of the wealthiest players, and de Peiresc one of the most learned. The Cardinal, with his taste and discernment, may have appreciated the Vase as a thing of beauty and historical curiosity, but for de Peiresc it meant much, much more.

De Peiresc was a scientist and historian, who collected books and manuscripts, and corresponded with nearly all the great minds of Europe, as if holding together by his letter-writing the entire intellectual community. He was driven by a desire to serve society by throwing light on the past, as his friend and biographer Gassendi described:

For the Fame and Memory of things, resembles the evening
Twilight, or shutting in of the day, which being at first
exceeding clear, does by little and little, in such sort vanish
away, as to be swallowed up in darkness; and therefore History
is needful, as a Torch, to bring the same to light.

De Peiresc had 'endeavoured to give light to the darkness of History'.
So he was among the first to value ancient artefacts because they
threw light on the world from which they came. Antiquities like the
Vase were not just curiosities or ornaments: they were vital pieces of
evidence.

An incident recorded by de Peiresc himself makes explicit the
divide between the wealthy collector and the scholar. In 1625, de
Peiresc was visited by a friend who was travelling with Cardinal
Barberini (who will come to figure more largely in the story of the
Vase). The friend brought de Peiresc a present, a set of ancient bronze
weights. De Peiresc had made a special study of ancient weights and
measures, and his friend must have hoped that his gift would go down
well. But de Peiresc modestly attempted to refuse it, telling his friend
the set should go to his patron. De Peiresc himself recounted how the
friend then 'reproached me that I render myself guilty in the eyes of
posterity of having deprived her of the fruits that could be extracted
from these fine pieces. That, moreover, it would be worth almost as
much to toss these into the sea as to give them to men of this sort.' So
much for the rich and powerful. De Peiresc sounds more in tune with
these democratic times than with the age of hereditary monarchy, and
for those of us who have not yet achieved either wealth or power his
is, of course, a consoling doctrine.

De Peiresc was born in Provence, at about the same time as the
Vase itself came to light. At the age of nineteen he travelled to Italy.
He trained as a lawyer, and he was interested in everything, from
astronomy to cat breeding, but his real passion was for antiquities. De

Peiresc was a collector, but of ideas as much as objects. This is how his biographer Gassendi describes his activities:

> He would carry about selected coins which he compared with the statues, seeking their date and type. He was such an expert that he knew immediately what was a genuine antiquity and what a copy. He wished to have copies of every ancient inscription, and he tried from his own knowledge to fill in the gaps and to restore the most hopeless texts ... He also noted everything which he deemed worthy of interest in the collections of metalwork and statuary, in the cabinets and the museums, in the galleries and various houses. In this way he brought together an extraordinary body of objects – by asking to borrow them, or by exchanging items, or receiving them as gifts, or by obtaining impressions, casts, fragments or drawings.

This is exactly what happened with the Vase. It was this dispassionate curiosity that brought de Peiresc to the Palazzo Madama, where he saw and examined the Vase, some time around 1600. Soon after, he got hold of a cast of it in lead (which he later passed on to the painter Rubens). He didn't want or need the real thing; he wanted knowledge. He didn't need to go digging; he found ample opportunity for his researches in the things that had already been found and collected. His role was to analyse, understand, and explain. For us who live in a world where the great treasures are kept in museums, open to all and curated by acknowledged experts, this attitude seems obviously right and proper, but in de Peiresc's time this was far from the case, as he himself made clear:

> Many people loudly scorn our studies, saying that they bring no glory to those who pursue them and no usefulness to others. The only ones who deserve such reproach are those who seek

scholarship of a meretricious sort, or even worse, content themselves with collecting antiquities to adorn their cupboards and decorate their their houses, only desiring them in order to be seen to possess them. On the other hand there are those who are entirely praiseworthy – they research the antiquities, study them and publish them in order to throw light on the works of the classical historians, to illustrate the unfolding of history, the better to impress upon the minds of men its personalities and their deeds, and great events.

If only de Peiresc had been at the opening of the Monte del Grano. One can't help thinking his account, and explanation, based on his methodical approach, would have been so much more convincing than the later claims of Girolamo Teti. But he wasn't, and anyway de Peiresc never actually published anything. We only know of his achievement through the writings of his biographer at the time, and from his own copious correspondence. His real legacy was the profound effect he had on the antiquarians who came after him, and all those who wanted 'to illustrate the unfolding of history'.

*

Cardinal Francesco Del Monte suffered a long, final illness during which he had ample leisure to decide where he might bestow his choice possessions. As a cleric he had of course no direct heirs, but there were plenty of family members clustered eagerly round the bedside. What would become of the Vase? In his will, Francesco had bequeathed it to someone denoted as 'Monsieur', who seems to have been the French prince who would become Henri II of Condé. But as the illness went on, the family went to work, and the will was changed. By the time Francesco died the Vase was safe in their hands. That these grieving relatives were not prompted by any deep-seated love of antiquities is demonstrated by the fact that, almost immediately, they sold the Vase on, for six hundred scudi.

So the Vase changed hands, and continued its journey down the river of history, its course following the currents of the great and the peculiar. It now passed from its first attested owner to the second, and the second is one of the very greatest and most peculiar that it would encounter in its long career. In 1627, after the death of Francesco, the Vase made a short journey from the Palazzo Madama to the Palazzo Barberini. This particular swirl of the current had at its centre Maffeo Barberini, known to posterity as Pope Urban VIII. The Vase's career as a top-flight status symbol was only just beginning, and far from being used to illuminate the past, it was about to be mixed up in the most excessive social posturing imaginable, not to mention black magic and murder.

Fifth Fragment
The Pope

The trouble with Urban VIII began at his election, and even by the standards of the Vatican it really was an extraordinary affair. The previous incumbent was Pope Gregory XV. He hadn't lasted long in office, but during his short reign he had effected one significant achievement: he had changed the rules by which Popes were elected.

Until Gregory, Popes were elected by a system known as acclamation, although 'system' is perhaps too dignified a term. A politically powerful cardinal would introduce his candidate to the conclave. He could do this at any moment, day or night; in the sight of his fellow cardinals he would simply say the words *ego eligo* – 'I choose *him*', and everyone would cheer (or boo and hiss). The candidate who inspired the loudest cheers was given the job, so cardinals would find themselves operating by a sort of herd mentality

– all stampeding to join in the cheering for fear of being left off the winning side.

Acclamation may be well suited for choosing the leader of a barbarian horde, but the Roman Catholic Church needed something a bit more sophisticated. Certainly Gregory was of this opinion, and wisely decreed that his successor would be chosen by secret ballot; then he promptly died. Everyone was thrown into confusion; the goal-posts had been moved. All the wheelers and dealers and power-brokers were caught out, so when the conclave sat to decide who should follow Gregory there was no backstage manoeuvring of the sort that had in the past made the proceedings a foregone conclusion. Popes had been chosen effectively by intrigue, but for the moment at least the secret ballot had put paid to that.

The conclave began on 19 July 1623, during a heat wave. There were two main contenders: Gregory's nephew, Cardinal Ludovico Ludovisi, and the nephew of the Pope-before-last, Cardinal Scipione Borghese. As ill-luck would have it they were very evenly matched; Gregory's reign had been so short that no party or clique had really had time to become dominant. We know from the similar proceedings of the juries of literary prizes that at this point a compromise candidate is usually introduced. But at first the factions belonging to the two nephews could not even agree on this. It was stalemate. The reactionaries began to shake their heads over this new-fangled ballot business, and some resolved to initiate a return to the good old days of election by pantomime-audience reaction. It took ten days of stifling heat and shortening tempers before a compromise candidate was finally suggested. Cardinal Maffeo Barberini was a popular choice. He belonged to neither faction, coming from a relatively obscure Florentine family, and had demonstrated extraordinary talents in the service of the church. He was also – so it is said – careful secretly to assure each faction that he was *on their side, really*. But Maffeo was only fifty-six – by papal standards a mere babe in arms. Older cardinals, of whom there were many, objected and it became clear that Maffeo was not going to get the two-thirds majority he needed. He bowed out.

Any summer spent in Rome was spent under the threat of malaria. By 3 August ten of the fifty-four cardinals present had gone down with it, as well as many of their secretaries and servants, some of whom began to leave. No fewer than eight cardinals and forty of their followers were to die of the disease over the summer. Things were getting truly desperate. A vacant See also meant a relaxation of law and order; the crime rate soared, and there was a sudden outbreak of headless bodies found lying in the street or floating in the Tiber. Prayers for divine intervention in the election process grew more and more heartfelt.

Under these circumstances, Maffeo was persuaded to re-enter the lists. Cardinal Scipione Borghese stood out against him, but now he himself went down with fever. On the morning of 6 August the votes were cast yet again, and Maffeo received forty-nine, a clear majority. But even as the word went out and a relieved city began to celebrate, it was discovered that one of the votes cast had gone missing. Pandemonium in the conclave. Maffeo himself called for a recount. The missing vote was found (according to one report a cardinal involved in the count and hostile to Maffeo had hidden it up his sleeve) and Maffeo was, finally, elected.

In this way a youngish man from a relatively obscure background suddenly found himself elevated to the papal throne. Maffeo's provincial, second-rank family, the Barberini, was in a single, giddy moment hoisted up above the old established Roman families. But how could the Barberini justify this revolution and cope with the attendant sense of inferiority? Maffeo found a rationale in the circumstances of his election. So chaotic, so out of control had the whole process been that surely no human agency was responsible for his election; instead, it was the hand of God Himself. God, in His mysterious way (secret ballots and malaria) had put him, Pope Urban VIII, above the Borghese, and the Colonna, and all the others; Maffeo ruled by divine right.

Having acquired, so he thought, heavenly backing, it only remained for Maffeo to assert his new status in the eyes of the world. He set about establishing the standing of his family by any and all means. Maffeo had an elder brother, Don Carlo, who had three sons, Francesco, Taddeo and Antonio. Brother Carlo and nephews Francesco and Antonio were made cardinals, and Maffeo invented the title 'eminence' for them. But Taddeo was singled out for even greater honour. His role would be to found a dynasty (the Pope himself, of course, being technically unable to produce an heir).

As Pope, Maffeo was not just the head of the Catholic Church: he was also the temporal ruler of the Papal States, with the income of this considerable territory at his disposal. He began to pour money into his nephews' pockets. Maffeo may not have invented nepotism, but according to contemporaries he certainly took it about as far as it could go. According to a contemporary diarist, 'avidity for accumulating wealth so blinded the Barberini nephews that night and day they thought of means to make themselves princes, how to render their family eternal, and how to redouble the filling of their storehouses.' It is calculated that during his pontificate Maffeo siphoned over a hundred million scudi into the family coffers, acquiring palaces, vineyards, pictures, statues, silver-work and gold, precious stones and, of course, one small but important antiquity. To give some idea of the worth of a scudo, the Vase cost the Barberini six hundred of them, and it was not cheap. But they had to have the Vase for the papal mantelpiece, and of course they had to have a palace to put the mantelpiece in.

In 1627 they began to build the Palazzo Barberini to demonstrate their new rank, and commissioned the foremost artists and sculptors to adorn it. A painted ceiling by Andrea Sacchi in the grandest conceivable manner illustrates the theme of divine election: a female figure representing Divine Wisdom sits enthroned and backed by a glorious sunburst. At her foot hangs the globe of the earth, with Italy at the top, illuminated by the sun's rays, and in shadow a rather speculative southern hemisphere, which of course had not yet been visited by Europeans. A programme in the family archives makes the theme of the painted ceiling explicit: 'Such a painting is appropriate to the majestic edifice of the Barberini family in order that it be understood that since that happy family was born and elected to rule the Church in the place of God it governs with Divine Wisdom, equally loved and revered.'

Taddeo Barberini had honours heaped upon him. At the age of twenty-three he was made lieutenant-general of the Church. The following year he married Anna Colonna, thus linking the Barberini with one of the most distinguished Roman families. At the age of twenty-eight he was made Prefect of Rome, a hereditary post with enormous social cachet. Maffeo, as paranoid parvenu, now insisted that his nephew took precedence over all other notables, including the foreign ambassadors who traditionally were accorded the status of the ruler they represented. In Rome at least, young Taddeo was a bigger fish than the King of France. It was stipulated that, according to his new standing, whenever Taddeo travelled through the streets of the city all other drivers must give way to his retinue of coaches. But the ambassadors simply refused to accept this, with fatal results.

According to the story, a few weeks after his investiture as prefect, Taddeo is making his progress through the city, when a wheel of his carriage gets caught in a rut. Coming up behind is the carriage of the Venetian ambassador, Giovanni Pesaro. According to the rules of precedence, Pesaro should pull over, but Rome and Venice have long been enemies, and instead he goes sailing past, diplomatic thumb to nose. Taddeo is infuriated. He gets in touch with Pesaro's coachman, and offers him a bribe if he will rein in the next time Taddeo passes.

It is not the principle of the thing, note, that interests Taddeo: it is merely the observation of precedence by any means, fair or foul. The coachman agrees to betray his master, and is promised reward and protection. Taddeo lurks outside the gates of the Venetian embassy, waiting for Pesaro, and a few days later, when Pesaro is returning from the Vatican, the clash occurs. Taddeo's coach approaches Pesaro's. The latter's coachman pretends to drop his hat, and pulls over as if to pick it up, but Pesaro realises what is going on. He jumps out, kicks the coachman off the box, seizes the reins and drives on.

Pesaro left the city in protest shortly after, and his coachman was found murdered, despite Taddeo's promise of protection. This unhappy story not only shows how driving in Rome has always been a risky activity; it also demonstrates just how obsessed the Barberini had become with status. The Venetian ambassador himself noted Maffeo's acquisitive posturing: 'Avidity for glory, the passion of great men, excessively agitates him, and he is always intent on those things that can aggrandise his personal image in the eyes of men and history.' Among those 'things', of course, was the Vase.

Now in the hands of a Pope, the Vase was witness to all the incidents and excesses of his reign. Maffeo Barberini, Pope Urban VIII, became notorious for many reasons. There was his extreme nepotism, and the greed of his nephews. There was his campaign to murder all the singing birds in his gardens because they disturbed his rest. There was another more costly and unsuccessful war that he began against the Farnese family in an attempt to wrest land from them, a war which drew his disparate enemies into an alliance against him, devastated the Papal States and exhausted their finances. Worst of all, perhaps, there was his poetry; Urban was excessively fond of literature, and liked nothing better than an afternoon spent with a select group of fellow authors in the Quirinal gardens (uninterrupted by birdsong), declaiming his dry, pedantic and utterly mediocre verses. He was opinionated, stubborn and so fond of the sound of his own voice that visiting ambassadors found themselves forced to listen to lengthy perorations on any and all subjects. One reported that he heard a weary cardinal mutter that now one gave an audience to the Pope, rather than the other way round. The Venetian ambassador discovered that with Maffeo's love of argument came a passion for contradiction, so much so that the wily ambassador developed the tactic of suggesting the opposite of his own desires, in order to gain their acceptance.

The distinguished historian Leopold von Ranke, whose *History of the Popes* records these foibles, uses an analogy to describe Maffeo's weakness which might give any writer pause for thought. Von Ranke condemns Maffeo as the kind of person who considers public office as chiefly a tribute to his own merit and personal importance:

Men thus constituted are far more powerfully influenced in the administration of their duties, by their own feelings and impulses, than by the exigencies of the case. They are not greatly dissimilar to an author, who, occupied by the consciousness of his talent, does not so much devote his thought to the subject before him as give free course to the caprices of his fancy.

So then, keeping rigidly to the subject before us: there are above all two scandals for which Maffeo is most notorious, and both involved men who studied the heavenly bodies. One was a private affair, secret and illicit. The other was almost certainly the greatest public embarrassment ever to befall the Catholic Church. Both can be traced directly to the overweening pride of Pope Urban VIII.

Sixth Fragment
Galileo Galilei and Tommaso Campanella

Just like Caravaggio's, Galileo Galilei's career was crucially helped by the influence of Cardinal Francesco del Monte. In 1588, thirty-five years before the election of Urban VIII, when the Vase was still in the hands of Cardinal del Monte, the twenty-four-year-old Galileo was trying to get a job at the university of Pisa. Del Monte had a brother, Guidobaldo, who was a mathematician of some ability, and had just published a definitive work on mechanics. Galileo found common ground with his noble colleague; they shared work on the gravity of solids. Through Guidobaldo, Galileo reached Cardinal Francesco, who could command the powerful interest of his own patron, the

Grand Duke. Between them, Francesco and Guidobaldo del Monte ensured that Galileo was offered a new post as junior lecturer at the university.

Having been launched on his career, Galileo continued to owe his advancement to the power of Cardinal Francesco del Monte, who helped him to achieve his next significant move, to the Chair of Mathematics at the University of Padua, then part of the Venetian Republic. Another member of the del Monte family was a general of the Venetian land forces, had played a hero's part in the wars of that powerful Republic, and was now responsible for its fortresses. General del Monte commissioned Galileo to write a tract on fortification, and the ambitious young man, scenting the financial rewards offered by defence contracts, was happy to comply. He invented a device to help artillerymen calculate the distance and height of their target, but it was the military potential of another invention which captivated the Venetian Senate.

Galileo did not invent the telescope, but he was perhaps the first to understand the implications of the device, particularly its military value, and he determined that he should be the one to bring it to fruition. He heard rumours of the development of the instrument in Holland, then that a Flemish craftsman had arrived in Padua itself, with a prototype, and was now – horror – already bound for Venice. This news galvanised him into frantic action. He resorted to his own workshop, and sought the services of a glass-blower.

The art of glass-blowing was invented during the early years of the Roman Empire, and one of the remarkable things about the Vase's construction is that this pinnacle of the ancient glass-blowers' art came only a few decades after the technique was developed. By Galileo's time the techniques of glass-blowing had hardly changed, but it was the artisans of the Venetian Empire who practised it now, in their workshops at Murano. One of these created different globes of glass for Galileo, from which were cut lenses. Galileo himself later claimed, perhaps not quite reliably, that in twenty-four hours he had worked out for himself the configuration of convex and concave lenses which would magnify objects at a distance. Stealing a march on his hapless Flemish competitor, Galileo presented his 'invention' to the Doge, the Council of Ten, and the commanders of the all-powerful Venetian navy.

The ruthless greybeards climbed the tower of St Mark's and one by one gazed through Galileo's spyglass. Suddenly the mouth of the Rio de Verieri, the river that served the glass-blowers of Murano, sprang clearly into view, though many miles distant. When they turned the telescope out to sea, the admirals could descry ships far out in the Adriatic. For the defence of a maritime power like Venice the implications of this new invention were obvious. The grateful Council voted Galileo a life salary – his fortune and his reputation were made. Galileo appreciatively despatched one of his first telescopes to del Monte, to join the Vase in his collection of curiosities.

But in his arrogance and his ambition, Galileo decided to leave the Venetians, despite their generous offer, for what he hoped would be the even more lucrative patronage of the Grand Duke in Florence, and he turned his telescope away from the sea-lanes and defences of the Venetian lagoon. In the autumn of 1609, standing on the top floor of his house in Padua, he looked at the Moon. Over the winter, through the clear night skies, he watched the silver disc wax and wane. At the same time he refined his instrument, doubling and redoubling its power. He gazed, fascinated, at the craters and the mountains, comparing the pitted lunar surface to a peacock's tail, and he made another analogy: the Moon resembled 'those glass vases which, while still hot, have been plunged into cold water and have thus acquired a crackled and wavy surface'. He saw the moons of Jupiter and the rings of Saturn, and he wrote *The Starry Messenger*, recording and analysing his findings. It became one of the most important books of the seventeenth century, and it decisively overthrew the Aristotelian view of the universe: the Sun did not go round the Earth. It also seemed directly to contradict several passages of scripture that described the movement of heavenly bodies, and thus brought Galileo into conflict with the Church.

In the Vatican a committee of clerics and theologians was convened to consider Galileo's findings, and rejected them as foolish and absurd: the Sun went round the Earth and that was that. Galileo was not to hold any other view, or teach it; he was to limit his researches to less dangerous matters. This setback took place in 1617, under Pope Paul V, long before the election of Urban VIII. Frustrated and dismayed, Galileo retreated, and forced himself to work on lesser, and less controversial, questions. He became involved in a debate about ice. His Aristotelian opponents asserted that ice was heavier than water, and only floated because of its flat, thin shape. Galileo reasoned that ice was lighter than the liquid form of water, and would float whatever its shape. A formal debate was organised at the Pitti Palace in Florence, and present was an up-and-coming cleric, Maffeo Barberini. Maffeo eagerly took Galileo's side, and watched with enthusiasm as Galileo routed his opponent. When Galileo sent Maffeo his tract on floating bodies, and his next work on sunspots, in reply Maffeo wrote effusively of the pleasure he would have in reading and re-reading Galileo's work. Maffeo was even moved to celebrate Galileo's achievement in nineteen stanzas of breathless verse. He called this ode *In Dangerous Adulation*.

When Maffeo was so unexpectedly elevated to the papal throne, Galileo was overjoyed. He travelled to Rome, and enjoyed an audience with Maffeo, who dispensed favour and approval. They even debated the old and new theories of the heavenly bodies, and Galileo came away with the impression that he could return to the forbidden subjects. He began a work intended to set out once and for all his thinking – a masterwork that would sum up the contending claims of the Aristotelian and Copernican systems. He couched it in the form of a dialogue: different characters would represent and discuss the different positions. By putting his ideas into the mouths of these characters, Galileo could keep his own views at one remove. He used the names of two old friends, Sagredo and Salviati, to denote his characters; these two were the sophisticates, who understood and espoused the new ideas. He added a third, an opponent who would state the case for the old established ideas of Aristotle: 'Simplicio'. Galileo finished his *Dialogue Concerning the Two Chief World Systems* in 1629, and in the spring of the following year, he brought the manuscript to Rome, and received provisional approval. In 1632 the first printed copies were in circulation. It was only now that Maffeo became familiar with the work. It threw him into a rage, and turned him from devoted, delighted fan to implacable enemy.

Galileo had made a dreadful error. Putting his arguments into a dialogue between advocates of the Copernican system and a defender of the Aristotelian meant that it was harder to hold him directly responsible for the dangerous new ideas being debated, but it was clear where his sympathies lay. It was also clear that in the debates Simplicio was the loser; as his name makes clear, he was the simpleton whose arguments were dismantled, and whose blunders were courteously explained and corrected. One of Simplicio's arguments was that however strong the scientific evidence might be, the human mind could not be certain of any interpretation, because an omnipotent God might have brought things about in a way beyond human understanding. This was a point which Maffeo himself had made, and, along with a hefty dose of paranoia and the memory of his personal interviews with Galileo, it was enough to convince him that Simplicio was intended for his own portrait. This was what enraged Maffeo; Galileo had been a friend, a recipient of admiring verses and benign patronage, and instead of showing his gratitude, he had taken advantage of Maffeo's indulgence and turned on his generous, unsuspecting friend, holding him up to ridicule.

Scholars wishing to protest against Urban's treatment of Galileo turned to none other than de Peiresc, relying on his acquaintance with Urban and Francesco Barberini. De Peiresc warned Francesco that the persecution of Galileo 'would run the risk of being interpreted and perhaps compared one day to the persecution of the person and wisdom of Socrates in his country, so condemned by other nations and by posterity itself'. This prophecy, entirely accurate, fell on deaf ears.

The whole repressive machinery of the Catholic Church ground into action. The Inquisition, the Jesuits, all those who felt threatened by Galileo's work, or had been subject to his arrogant and devastating put-downs, could now gleefully assist at his destruction. But Galileo's trial, his interrogation, the threats of torture, his forced confession and public recantation, the seizure and destruction of his books and the sentence of imprisonment, his subsequent life under house arrest and above all the fatal damage done to the progress of learning and science in Italy – all this can be traced directly to the wounded vanity of Maffeo Barberini.

*

It is something of an irony that while Maffeo condemned Galileo's heretical theories, he himself harboured far more dangerous ideas concerning the heavenly bodies. Maffeo was addicted to astrology, firmly believing that the influence of the planets could drastically affect life on Earth. He identified himself with the Sun. At the time of his dramatic and unforeseen election, the Sun had been in conjunction with Jupiter, a confirmation of the Divine Will. The Sun was his sign, prominent in his astrological birth-chart as 'Lord of the Ascendant' and 'Giver of Life', and it became the badge of his papacy. The head of Apollo, the Sun god, appears on the façade of the Palazzo Barberini. Maffeo decorated his Vatican apartments with a picture of the rising Sun so that this auspicious image would greet him when he opened his eyes in the morning. According to the Venetian ambassador at the time, despite the fact that he had forbidden anyone else to study it, Maffeo's knowledge of astrology was profound, and his every move was dictated by what he saw in the stars.

The practice of astrology was common enough at the time, but Maffeo went further than merely accommodating his actions to astrological phenomena. Subject to all the superstitious terrors inherent in his beliefs, he resorted to magical practices. Soon after he was elected in 1623, in order to over-awe his cardinals Maffeo began to cast their horoscopes, asserting that he could predict the time of their deaths. This tactic backfired badly: astrologers were promptly commissioned by his victims to draw up *his* horoscope, and speculate about *his* death, and some of them began to suggest that this unfortunate event might be imminent. As well as the desire for a fitting revenge there were serious political motives behind this: the Spanish, who disapproved of Maffeo's sympathy for their great rival France, were trying to stir up trouble. They even pretended to prepare for another conclave, apparently so certain of the truth of the predictions that they sent their cardinals to Rome in eager anticipation of Maffeo's demise and the election of a new Pope. Rumours spread, and began to be believed.

Maffeo issued a somewhat hypocritical Bull forbidding the astrological prediction of the demise of the Pope, on pain of death. He had an abbot called Morandi, a keen student of the occult, put on trial for compiling a birth-chart for the Pope. Morandi was imprisoned and quietly poisoned. Another victim of this crackdown was the nephew of Cardinal Felice Centini. Believing through astrological prediction that his uncle would become the next Pope, and desiring to hasten this happy event, Giacinto Centini performed the Black Mass and a ceremony involving a wax effigy of Maffeo in order to kill him by witchcraft. He was put to death for this crime. Maffeo even took steps to conceal the date of his birth, to prevent more birth-charts being drawn-up. But the damage had been done; if the Spanish intended to scare Maffeo, they succeeded. Indeed it could be said that they nearly frightened him to death, because Maffeo truly believed in the influence of the heavens, for good and ill, and a whole string of perilous astrological events were fast approaching. In January 1628 there was to be an eclipse of the Moon, in December of the same year an eclipse of the Sun, and then another in June 1630. The solar eclipse in particular filled Maffeo with real dread; during it his sign would be darkened and, left unprotected, he would be threatened by all the inimical powers of the heavens. He needed protection, and in his desperation he turned to a most unlikely source in the person of an eccentric Friar and notorious millennarian called Tommaso Campanella.

Campanella had been tortured and imprisoned in Naples for his heretical and revolutionary ideas, which centred on a belief in the imminent approach of the Sun to the Earth, and hopes of a Utopian society. He had been involved in a revolt in Calabria, and only avoided the death penalty on a plea of insanity. After many years in prison he was released and made his way to Rome, where he was again incarcerated, in 1626. But in 1628 rumours began to circulate that, at liberty again, he had been performing black magic rituals – 'nocturnal rites with lighted candles' – and that his companion in this dangerous mischief was Maffeo himself.

Campanella derived his rites from a predecessor, the fifteenth-century magus Marsilio Ficino, who believed that a Cosmic Spirit flowed through the universe, permeating all things, and that it was through the action of this Spirit that heavenly bodies affected the Earth. Ficino believed that this Spirit could be attracted and as it were focused by appropriate actions and objects: food, scents, plants, music and certain talismans, properly deployed, might attract a benign influence or turn aside a malign power. Campanella adapted these beliefs to suit the anxieties of his new patron, and devised a magical ceremony to protect Maffeo from the dangers of an eclipse.

Naturally, Campanella kept these practices secret, but he made the mistake of writing them down. When he submitted a six-volume work on astrology to a publisher in Paris, it seems that some of his enemies got hold of the secret treatise, and added it to the rest without his knowledge. The final work came out in seven volumes and the final volume described Campanella's magical rites for the eclipse. This cunning piece of malice proved highly effective; Campanella was bewildered to see his mysteries in print, and Maffeo was infuriated by what he saw as a breach of trust, and commissioned spies to keep Campanella under observation and ensure that he did not betray any more embarrassing secrets. However, the long term effect of this publication has been to give us a fascinating glimpse of what went on in the Palazzo Barberini in June 1630, when the eclipse threatened, and the terrified Pope sought Campanella's aid.

A room was prepared, hung with white silk draperies, and decorated with the signs of the Zodiac. Maffeo and Campanella dressed themselves in white robes. As the eclipse approached, this room was sealed against its pestiferous influence. The heavenly bodies were represented within the room by candles or torches. Strong-scented essences like rose-vinegar were sprinkled about, and aromatic herbs – rosemary, laurel and myrtle – were burnt. These were to guard against the pestilential elements spreading under the darkness of the eclipse, and in particular the evil influence of Mars and Saturn, which could operate unchecked when the Sun was dimmed. Stones, plants and colours associated with benign planets, Jupiter and Venus, were deployed, to attract their protection. Music associated with these planets was performed discreetly, while Maffeo drank specially distilled liquors.

The music played, pungent scents wafted about, the candles burned, the smoke of the burning herbs drifted up, wreathing amongst a row of talismans, perhaps around the Vase itself, and Maffeo sipped his prophylactic drink in perfect safety. Strange to say, he emerged from his ordeal with his life-force miraculously unharmed, and doubtless in his relief he gratefully ascribed his survival to the efficacy of the measures devised by his necromantic adviser.

Did the Vase oversee these bizarre goings-on? It would be nice to think so, and we have solid proof that the Vase was in the Barberini Palace at this period. Now for the first time careful drawings were made of the Vase, as it remained in the keeping of Maffeo and his family. This earliest attempt to record the Vase was the work of another member of the Barberini entourage, Cassiano dal Pozzo, whose activities were more down-to-earth but in their way every bit as remarkable as those of the eccentric Campanella. Anticipating its fate by several hundred years, dal Pozzo decided that the Vase properly belonged in a Museum, and determined to put it there.

Seventh Fragment
Cassiano dal Pozzo and the Barberini

Cassiano dal Pozzo moved in the same dangerous circles as Galileo, and became a close friend; like Galileo, he was a member of the Accademia dei Lincei, or lynxes, the ancestor of all scientific societies. It was founded by the wealthy and powerful young nobleman, Prince Federico Cesi, in 1603, and to begin with had only four members. They were all young, single men, dedicated to scientific investigation. Galileo, whose new telescope delighted the lynx-eyed academicians, became the fifth member in 1611. Dal Pozzo himself joined about a decade later.

Dal Pozzo, again like Galileo, had befriended the Barberini family before Maffeo's unforeseen elevation to the papacy, and he reaped the benefits of this association. When Maffeo's nephew Francesco Barberini was made a cardinal, dal Pozzo was given a position in his household and a comfortable income. He advised Francesco, who was keen to bestow his patronage, but not himself blessed with the keenest of intellects. Dal Pozzo travelled on diplomatic missions with Francesco to Paris and Madrid, and although the missions were in diplomatic terms miserable failures, they allowed Francesco to indulge his growing passion for the arts, and cemented his regard for dal Pozzo's learning and cultivation. Dal Pozzo thus became one of the most influential individuals in the cultural life of Rome. He was not interested in enriching himself, as we know from his father's plaintive letters, urging him to take more advantage of the favour he enjoyed with the Barberini. He contented himself with his relatively moderate income, and spent all his time and money on science and learning. In this he seems admirable, certainly when compared to his grasping and extravagant patrons, and he certainly gained the respect of other scholars, corresponding for instance with de Peiresc, but he does seem to have been a rather cold and reserved personality. There is a caricature of him, drawn by Bernini, which captures an ill-tempered profile, a bristling moustache, a bull-neck and double chin, and something rather choleric about the eye.

He began to collect: rare birds and plants, mechanical instruments, medals, precious stones, sculptures, books and paintings. Dal Pozzo could not aspire to the priceless objects that adorned the Palazzo Barberini; he was not the kind of player who could afford the Vase. But nor was his collection merely a heap of curiosities; it was arranged, categorised, and presented for the furtherance of knowledge and scientific understanding.

When the chief Lynx, Prince Cesi, died in 1630, dal Pozzo eagerly acquired some of his books and scientific equipment. Unfortunately, Cesi's death marked the start of the Academy's decline. Without his power and influence, the members were left exposed to the forces of reaction, with Galileo as the first spectacular victim. Dal Pozzo tactfully turned his attention away from natural science to a safer area of study – that of antiquities. But he still tackled his subject with the rigorous systematic approach that the Academy of the Lynxes had fostered in him, determining to make a record of every surviving trace of Ancient Rome that he could find. He bought existing drawings and commissioned artists to go out and make new records of antiquities wherever they could be found in the city. The guiding principle, moreover, was not simply to capture and celebrate the beauty of statues, sculptures and inscriptions: dal Pozzo wanted to piece things together, to gain as broad an understanding of the past as possible.

He collated these drawings into a vast work of twenty-three volumes. He called it his *Museum Chartaceum* – his Paper Museum – and in it the drawings were arranged by subject matter. Volume I contained images relating to religious beliefs and practices (cautiously described as 'False', just in case some zealous Jesuit decided to accuse him of paganism). Volume II dealt with marriage, clothes, theatrical spectacles and baths, and Volume IV contained statues, utensils and vases. Naturally the Vase itself took pride of place in this gallery of the Museum. Six drawings of the Vase were included in the Paper Museum, some of which, like the Vase itself, are now preserved in the British Museum.

One of the artists whom dal Pozzo commissioned to provide the entries for his Paper Museum was a young Parisian living in Rome, called Nicolas Poussin. The employment was a profound and lasting influence on Poussin, who breathed in at every pore the spirit of the classical world from his detailed study of antiquities for the Museum. Dal Pozzo for his part realised that in Poussin he had an artist who was uniquely disposed to understand and revive that spirit. There is some testimony, from an eighteenth-century English visitor to Italy who claimed to have seen it, that Poussin made a painting of the Vase for dal Pozzo, although any such work has long been lost. Dal Pozzo did commission more than fifty paintings from Poussin, in particular the *Seven Sacraments*, a cycle of paintings portraying the rites of the Church – marriage, confirmation, ordination, and so on – as performed in its earliest days. These revolutionary paintings (which will figure again in the history of the Vase) show dal Pozzo's interest in the past, and also suggest some unorthodox religious views. Living as it were in the pocket of the religious Establishment, dal Pozzo was not well placed to exhibit symptoms of such beliefs, but it appears that he was far from conventional in his thinking. There is the curious case of Jean-Jacques Bouchard, an unbeliever and *libertin*, who bequeathed his private papers to his good friend dal Pozzo. What dal Pozzo thought of these is not recorded, but he showed them to another, more conventional friend, who was shocked by 'filth' and 'devilish things'. As we know, Dal Pozzo was not only drawn to the early practices of the Christian Church; he also showed a keen interest in the pagan rites of the Ancient Romans, as his Museum volume dedicated to such 'False' practices demonstrates. The inference is that he viewed both pagan and Christian with an equally learned and sceptical eye.

Some of the drawings of the Vase that made up the entry in dal Pozzo's Museum are now kept in the Royal Library at Windsor. They are a careful study of the whole frieze, laid out in a rectangular composition, done in black chalk. They have been ascribed to a close friend of Poussin's, Pietro Testa. Testa was certainly one of the artists whom dal Pozzo employed, along with Poussin, to make drawings of the ancient reliefs and sculptures, but he does not seem to have enjoyed the task as much as Poussin, and fell foul of dal Pozzo's authoritarian approach. When Testa lost patience with the work of copying and tried to escape from his employment, Dal Pozzo had him thrown into jail for breach of contract. Testa went on to attempt a career as a painter on the grand scale, but met with no success, and eventually drowned himself in the Tiber.

Dal Pozzo, like his colleague and correspondent de Peiresc, was another of those who appreciated the Vase without owning it. His influence as a patron and arbiter of taste was inevitably tied to the fortunes of his patrons. Although he continued his scholarly activities in private until his death in 1657, his life at the centre of power and wealth came to an end with the fall of the Barberini, which was every bit as spectacular as their original rise.

*

Maffeo Barberini reigned as Pope Urban VIII for more than twenty years, and the longer his hold on power lasted, the more unpopular he and his family became. Nepotism was an accepted part of life in the Vatican, but Maffeo took it to such an extreme, siphoning such colossal sums into the pockets of his family, that even the cynical Romans grew outraged. He also raised more and more taxes to shore up the finances of the Church, which, after a long history of maladministration, were already in a parlous state. He did not scruple to tax basic commodities, including corn, and this turned popular opinion firmly against him. Finally, he embarked on his disastrous war against the Farnese family, who owned a princedom neighbouring the Papal States. Relations between the Pope and Duke Odoardo Farnese soured when on a visit to Rome the Duke refused to bow to Taddeo Barberini, or pay his respects to Antonio Barberini. Garrisons were reinforced, economic sanctions were applied, until the dispute escalated into all-out war. Taddeo marched out of Rome on the offensive, but Farnese raised an army, defeated Taddeo, and threatened the City itself. Eventually a peace treaty was signed, with terms overwhelmingly favourable to the Duke. Huge sums had been squandered on the war, serious damage had been done to the lands over which it had been fought and the Barberini had been clearly worsted. Only a few months after the peace treaty was signed in 1644, seventy-six-year-old Maffeo, disappointed and defeated, took to his bed to die. His conscience finally pricking him, he summoned his advisers to his bedside and asked them if, perhaps, he had been slightly too generous towards his family. The throng of sycophants reassured him that he had behaved with perfect propriety, but when news of his death was announced, a happy populace pulled down his statues. Worse still, in the ensuing conclave, the successful papal candidate, despite the best efforts of the Barberini faction, was Giambattista Pamphili, known for his opposition to Maffeo's nepotism and the disastrous war. He became Pope Innocent X, and immediately took steps to arraign the remaining Barberini. Antonio, Francesco and Don Taddeo and his family all fled to Paris. Innocent was forced to content himself with confiscating their possessions and shutting up their palaces.

What then of the Vase? It was left in the care of Taddeo's wife Anna. She alone stayed behind in Rome to defend the interests of the family as best she could. Somehow, despite Innocent's strictures, she managed to hang on to the family treasures. When Francesco, Antonio and Taddeo arrived in Paris, they sought the protection of the chief minister, the all-powerful Mazarin, and eventually this man forced Innocent to accept the return of the Barberini. Only a few years after their flight, they reappeared in Rome, magically repossessed of their wealth and status (except for Taddeo, who had died in Paris). The dynasty and its fortune survived. By 1653, the family were once more taking an ostentatious part in the city's festivities; the theatre in the Palazzo Barberini was re-opened, and tickets offered to the public. The following year Taddeo's son, the Prince of Palestrina, appeared in the carnival parade on a float drawn by four horses. He was dressed as the Sun, seated on a throne, accompanied by four horsemen representing the seasons, and by a hundred young men in gold costumes carrying torches symbolising the solar rays. The Barberini were back, and they had come to stay; despite all obstacles Maffeo's dynastic ambitions had paid off, and the Vase remained in their possession.

Despite their triumphant recovery, over the next few decades the Barberini followed the fate of all the Roman aristocracy: that is, they slipped into a slow but inexorable decline. The aristocracy had for generations supported itself on what were known as *monti*, shares issued by the State which paid an annual yield of about five per cent. This yield lasted for ever, and could be sold or inherited. Those who could afford to own these shares were thus provided with a sort of everlasting pension, which removed the need to invest in, say, agriculture, or indeed any kind of enterprise. Paying the interest on these shares came to absorb a significant proportion of the revenues of the State; at the time of the Vase's discovery at the end of the sixteenth century, this proportion had already reached about sixty per cent. The money that poured into Rome from the sale of offices and other revenues of the Catholic Church was often spent on distributing food for the poor, and even on dowries for underprivileged young women. None of this encouraged an entrepreneurial spirit or a healthy economy. The Papal States were exceptional in that they were run by clerics, and although these may have fostered the spiritual well-being of their subjects, they were poorly qualified to audit the finances. Worse, this theocracy, funded by the enormous riches of the Church, indulged in luxurious living and lavish display. The aristocracy as a whole could not help competing, and often did so by running into debt. The Barberini, as the Prince of Palestrina's extravagant carnival-float demonstrates, were no exception. Without Maffeo to channel millions of scudi into the family coffers, slowly but surely their fortunes dwindled.

But as the Barberini family decayed, the fame of the Vase grew, and so did the number of interpretations of the figures on it, and so did the startling contradictions between these different theories. In 1690, one Michel-Ange Caseo de La Chausse published his *Romanum Museum sive Thesaurus Eruditae Antiquitatis*, which contains both illustration and explanation of the Vase. At first, de La Chausse limits himself to one side only, that is to say figures A-D. He believes that this scene tells the story of the birth of Alexander the Great. His clue is figure C – the lady with the snake. According to his theory she is Alexander's mother Olympias; there is a myth that tells how she was visited by Jupiter in the form of a snake, and that the result of this meeting was Alexander himself. Figure D is Jupiter in his proper form, as it were surveying his handiwork. Figure A is described by de La Chausse as a 'Genius'. In the classical world there was a belief that everyone had a spirit, or genius, who had influence over an individual's nature and character; this is such a figure. Although de La Chausse does not specify to whom this spirit belongs, perhaps it is to Alexander himself, who is about to be, or has just been, or is in the process of being conceived, by the reclining lady and her serpent, whose up-reared attitude now takes on new connotations.

What then of Cupid, flying above Olympias, and seeming to beckon Alexander's genius on? De La Chausse makes no remark. Nor does he deal with the other side of the Vase, until his Erudite Thesaurus is reprinted in 1746, when the three figures E, F and G are identified as the Muses. The Muses, however, were all female, so this interpretation is undermined by the appearance of figure E, whose manly chest and male genitalia, carelessly revealed by the drapery that hangs across the lap, hint that perhaps figure E at least is not one of the Muses after all.

So de La Chausse (who turns out like his predecessor to be either rather cavalier about the sexing of the figures or just chronically short-sighted) can hardly be regarded as having cleared the matter up once and for all, and we cannot be surprised to find that only seven years after the publication of the Erudite Thesaurus, another theory appears. This was formulated by Pietro Santo Bartoli, the very same writer who gave us the unreliable description of the finding of the tomb in the Monte del Grano; let us not hold this against him, but rather judge his case on its merits.

Bartoli strikes out in an entirely new direction, linking the figures to the myth of Proserpina. She is the daughter of Ceres, goddess of agriculture, and when not helping her mother with the harvest she likes to idle away the time picking flowers on the island of Sicily with a train of nymphs. One day, their singing and laughter attracts the attention of Pluto, god of the Underworld. Pluto drives about in a chariot drawn by four black horses, carrying a two-pronged spear with which he can strike and remove any obstacle in his path. Pluto's gloomy character is in part due to his misfortunes in love; none of the goddesses would agree to be his bride and live in the infernal courts of Hades, and in fact he suffered so many refusals that he had sworn never to ask again. This perhaps explains, though it does not excuse, his actions in this tale; having spied on the beautiful young Proserpina from a nearby thicket, he bursts out, seizes the hapless goddess, drags her back to his chariot, whips up his coal-black steeds, and gallops away. To evade pursuit, he strikes the ground with his spear, opening a crevasse and disappearing down into the land of the dead. Ceres, missing her daughter, wanders the world vainly seeking her and letting the harvest rot, until Jupiter takes pity on her, and decrees that Proserpina should be allowed to return to her mother if she has eaten nothing during her stay in the Underworld. But it emerges that Proserpina has nibbled six pomegranate seeds in her captivity, and so Jupiter decides that for six months of the year Proserpina must return to Pluto's side.

Bartoli maintains that figure C is Proserpina, and figure E Pluto, and figure G Proserpina again, but this is hardly satisfactory. What of the snake, of Cupid and all the other figures on the Vase? Where is Pluto's two-pronged fork, or the pomegranate, or Ceres? What prompted this theory in the first place? Figure F, with her up-ended torch, the fallen capital at her feet suggests, perhaps, death. Bartoli's interpretation, however, is disappointingly cursory; he is the first of the merely slap-dash theoreticians, who content themselves with identifying one or two figures only. It is hardly a satisfactory approach.

The next contender is Bernard de Montfaucon, who published his *L'Antiquité Expliquée* in 1722, and unfortunately was another of the same cursory stamp. He attempts to identify only two figures, C and D. In order to do so, he selects yet another myth from the inexhaustible catalogue – that of Leda and the swan. In this myth, the god Jupiter falls in love with Leda, wife of the King of Sparta. Jupiter, who is endowed with all-too-human passions, conducts many liaisons and, often arousing the jealous rage of his wife Juno, makes a habit of assuming some disguise before having his way with whichever nymph or mortal woman catches his eye. He ravishes Europa, the daughter of King Agenor, by assuming the form of a bull and carrying her off on his broad back. When Juno catches him out with Io, the daughter of a river-god, he quickly changes the nymph herself into a beautiful heifer (unfortunately Juno sees through this ruse, and sends a gadfly to plague the heifer to madness). In the same fashion Jupiter assumes the disguise of a swan in order to ravish the mortal woman Leda. Leda then gives birth to the twin heroes Castor and Pollux, and subsequently to Helen, whose face will launch a thousand ships to the siege of Troy.

De Montfaucon identifies figure C as Leda, and D as Jupiter. He does not try very hard with the rest: 'It is not easy to discover what the other figures are doing', he notes, without pausing to wonder whether this might cast his theory into doubt, 'nor what relation there is between this fable and the ashes of Alexander Severus. Perhaps it is best to say that the first precious vessel which came to hand was made use of for this purpose.' De Montfaucon's theory is not only incomplete, it also seems to be based on a serious misapprehension, that the creature rearing up beside figure C is the swan, or rather Jupiter in swan's form. If the creature caressed by figure C had been a giraffe or a rhinoceros, something that de Montfaucon himself had never seen, or a mythical creature, about whose appearance he could only guess, perhaps we could forgive him. But a *swan*? Perhaps de Montfaucon knew of the myth as Leda and the Snake, or perhaps, like so many of those before and after him, he ventured into print without having actually looked closely at the Vase at all.

In 1756 Ridolfino Venuti published his *Spiegazione de' bassirilievi che si osservano nell' urna sepolcrale detta d'Alessandro Severo*. He hit on the myth of the Judgement of Paris to explain the frieze. In this story, the goddess of discord, having failed to receive her invitation to the marriage of Peleus and Thetis, turns up anyway, and throws an apple onto the table labelled 'For the Fairest'. The three chief goddesses – Venus, Minerva and Juno – all lay claim to it, and appeal to Jupiter. He, being no fool, decides that a lucky mortal, Paris, Prince of Troy, shall make the decision. The goddesses duly parade before Paris, who is at this time living as a shepherd on Mount Ida, and dangle appropriate bribes: Minerva offers wisdom, Juno offers power and Venus offers the favours of the most beautiful woman in the world, i.e. Helen, daughter of Leda. Venuti identifies figure A as Paris, C as the goddess of discord, who, 'as if thrown out of heaven, sits on earth', fondling a serpent to symbolise her tricksy nature, and D as Jupiter. On the other side, the rocks on which the three figures sit represent Mount Ida, and the figures themselves are the goddesses. This theory would fit better if the three figures were female, but Venuti, like his predecessors, shows some confusion in the matter of gender, and endows figure E, who he takes to be Venus, goddess of love, with male genitalia.

This might seem a bewildering array of theories, but it was just the beginning, a mere trickle of scholarly hypotheses that would gradually swell to a flood. They all served to inflate the reputation of the Vase. More and more visitors were coming to the Palazzo Barberini to admire it. By the time Venuti published his theory in the mid-eighteenth century, the Vase had become an acknowledged stop on the Grand Tour.

Eighth Fragment
Johann Winckelmann and James Byres

Mother dabs away a tear, Father claps you on the shoulder and shouts a last command to your tutor, John the coachman folds up the steps and jumps onto the box, and you are off in a cloud of dust down the road to Dover. Your belongings are strapped up behind in a great mass of trunks and bundles: tinderbox and tea-caddy, handkerchiefs and hats, penknife and passport-holder. You clutch your guidebook, with its lists of questions to ask, places to visit and works of art to view. Dover to Calais, Calais to Paris, down through France and over the Alps to Italy; you are off on the Grand Tour, an established part of every young eighteenth-century aristocrat's education, a finishing-school in which you are supposed to acquire languages, grace of address, broader horizons, self-reliance and taste. Putting up at noxious inns and being fleeced by the innkeeper, bribing your way through the innumerable customs-houses, fighting off vermin, beggars and banditti, gawping at foreign customs and clothes, bridling at unfamiliar and garlic-laden food, facing the terrors of the mountains and the heat of the plains, until at last, having braved the Simplon Pass (where your faithful King Charles spaniel is eaten by wolves) and the rapacious douaniers and appalling roads of Piedmont, your carriage tops a rise, and you behold the roofs, towers, steeples and domes of the Eternal City, furthest and foremost destination of everyone who ever went on the Tour.

In Rome you take rooms (cheap and generously proportioned for less than six guineas a month), browse the shops (watchmakers on the Piazza Capranica, booksellers around the Chiesa Nuova), venture down into the catacombs, and have your portrait painted by Pompeo Batoni, standing proudly in front of the Colosseum. If you have arrived before Easter, you enjoy the spectacle of the carnival, and the solemn ceremony during which the Pope washes the feet of twelve selected aged pilgrims. But most of all, you are here to view the antiquities, to pick your way through the maze of ruins – columns, obelisks, arches and temples, often obscured by weeds and rubbish, but beside which you may attempt to bring to life the verses of Horace or the noble periods of Caesar that were beaten into you in childhood. Dutifully you take notes as your tutor holds forth, and dutifully you tick off the stops in your guidebook. The sights are inexhaustible; how long you are prepared to spend on them depends on your own enthusiasm and stamina. Dr John Moore, in his *View of Society and Manners in Italy*, describes the behaviour of a fellow countryman, who did not want to spend every afternoon trailing round the sights, but still wanted to claim that he had, so to speak, got the t-shirt:

He ordered a post-chaise and four horses to be ready early in the morning, and driving through churches, palaces, villas, and ruins, with all possible expedition, he fairly saw, in two days, all that we had beheld during our crawling course of six weeks. I found afterwards, by the list he kept of what he had done, that we had not the advantage of him in a single picture, or the most mutilated remnant of statue.

For all eighteenth-century visitors, high-speed or snail's pace, fascinated or bored, the Vase, still displayed in the palace of the surviving though now much reduced Barberini family, had become a must-see. For any tour that would include the most important highlights, a guide was needed, a local expert. Pick of the bunch was Johann Joachim Winckelmann, eminent German antiquarian.

Winckelmann had acquired his knowledge the hard way. Born in utter poverty, the only child of a Prussian cobbler, he worked his passage through school and university, drudging as classroom assistant and private tutor. Unable to afford books, he developed the habit of borrowing works and copying extracts in order to create his own library. After university he worked for five years as a teacher in a school in the provincial town of Seehausen. After a day spent teaching, he would study until midnight, sleep in his chair until four, then wake and study again. He was also giving private lessons to a young man living with him, whom he had tutored, and who had followed him to Seehausen. Winckelmann was certainly gay, and extant letters from him to this room-mate are full of endearments, but even if there was more to this relationship than meets the eye, it's hard to see how he would have had the leisure to enjoy it much. Winckelmann, according to his sentimental nineteenth-century biographer, Carl Justi, like a slave, only half belonged to himself in the day. His real life began at night, when he invited the ancients to be his guests. There he sat, the pale and lean man, in his narrow, bare, ice-cold cell, with his dark, sparkling eyes peering out from the depths of his cloak into a parchment copy of Plutarch or Sophocles, dreaming, in the midst of impenetrable, snow-covered fields, of the Mediterranean and its people.

Slowly, and with great pains, he clawed his way up the ladder of employment. He landed a job as research assistant to a court official in Saxony, who was compiling a history of the German Empire. Winckelmann was given the deadly task of checking dates for this massive, turgid tome. But the work gave him access to a large library, which he was then given the task of cataloguing. He taught himself English, and copied excerpts from Pope and Milton (and delighted in Cleland's *Fanny Hill*). But in his studies he inclined more and more to the world of Ancient Greece, and to Greek art in particular. He determined that this should be his life's work. From his reading and dreaming he developed a vision of Ancient Greece as a utopia, producing ideal forms of 'noble simplicity and quiet grandeur'. It is an idea that has embedded itself in our consciousness.

While working in the library, he came into contact with Count Alberigo Archinto, Papal Nuncio to the Court of Saxony. Archinto saw his qualities, and gave Winckelmann his golden chance – to work as librarian to Archinto's friend Cardinal Passionei in Rome. The cobbler's son became librarian to His Eminence the Cardinal Secretary of State, with an apartment in the Palazzo della Cancelleria. Once settled in the Eternal City, Winckelmann began to study the antiquities stored there, and to gather materials for his *History of Ancient Art*. He also felt more sexual freedom; Casanova recounted a story of catching him *in flagrante* with a young man, at which

Winckelmann explained he was only indulging in homosexuality in order to imitate the Ancient Greeks.

In 1763 the cobbler's son was appointed Papal Antiquary by Pope Clement XIII. Winckelmann had a salary, a great deal of prestige, and only a moderate amount of official duties. One of these was to keep track of antiquities and make sure they were not being smuggled out of the country – but there were troops of underlings to take care of this. Winckelmann's real task was to take any prominent visitors who expressed an interest on a tour of the city; he was now hobnobbing with the rich and powerful. Bishop, milord, diplomat, statesman, all were to be charmed, informed and entertained, their foibles or drunkenness ignored, and their demands for erotic satisfaction tactfully passed on to 'Viscioletta', a top-ranking courtesan of the day. The Duke of York, brother to George III, was escorted by Winckelmann, who described him as 'the greatest idiot I know'. Writer James Boswell and demagogue John Wilkes both enjoyed his company (Wilkes had a mistress in tow, and their guide sometimes had to turn a blind eye when the besotted pair seized an opportunity to retire to a secluded corner of the church or palazzo and enjoy each other's company). One morning, Winckelmann complained, he had the Prince of Mecklenburg, the Prince of Anhalt-Dessau, and the Duc de La Rochefoucauld 'each of them desiring me to spend the day with them alone'.

Winckelmann must have seen the Vase often enough in the Barberini Palace as he showed it off to his distinguished guests, and he developed his own theory as to the meaning of the figures. He identified figure A as Peleus, and figure C as the beautiful sea-nymph Thetis, daughter of the sea-god Nereus. (This identification depends on the serpent which she is fondling; Winckelmann, one of the few who seems to have examined the figures closely, saw the fan-shaped fin hanging from the creature's throat, and the small fins on the back of its neck, and determined quite reasonably that this was a sea-serpent.) Backed by a life's work of intense study of classical literature and art, his theory has an excellent pedigree, and is worth looking at in some detail.

The story of Peleus and Thetis begins when Neptune and Jupiter both fall for the lovely nymph. Any rivalry is quickly curbed when Themis, goddess of order, prophesies that when Thetis gives birth to a son, he shall be greater than his father. At the prospect of siring an heir more powerful than themselves, both the gods step swiftly back, and agree that Thetis must be married to a mortal so that she will not produce some powerful young godling capable of supplanting them. Themis suggests the hero Peleus, who sailed with Jason on the quest for the Golden Fleece. Thetis, however, has not been consulted, and does not acquiesce. According to one version of the myth, when Peleus makes his suit to the nymph and embraces her, she resists him by changing her shape, so that the hero finds in his arms a lion, then a snake, then a raging fire, and so on. Peleus, however, has been warned by his friend Chiron the centaur that something of the sort might happen, and Chiron has advised him that if he holds on long enough, Thetis will return to her proper form, and submit to his advances. This proves to be the case; after the vigorous and successful wooing, the gods themselves grace the wedding-feast, and at length Thetis bears a baby son who will become the greatest of all mortal heroes – Achilles.

But of course there is no sign of a wrestling match on the Vase, no clutching and shape-shifting, only a calm and decorous scene in which Cupid leads the suitor towards an entirely acquiescent-looking nymph; how then does the theory stand up? There is another version of the myth, in which Thetis is brought up by Juno, wife to Jupiter, and when Jupiter courts her, she rejects him out of loyalty to her guardian. Jupiter, frustrated and annoyed, decrees that Thetis shall be married to a mortal. Juno, however, makes sure that the mortal is the finest then living – the hero Peleus. As he is Juno's choice, Thetis makes no protest, but accepts the match. This version certainly accords better with the figures on the first side of the Vase. Figure A is Peleus, approaching his intended, but looking anxiously over her head at figure D, Jupiter, who gives his approval. This less violent version is celebrated by the Roman writer Catullus, who describes in highly sensual and romantic terms in his Poem 64 how Peleus sees and falls for Thetis. From the deck of the *Argo*, he and the other Argonauts look down into the water, and see Thetis and the other daughters of Nereus:

> As soon as the *Argo* cleared with her prow the windswept sea and the oar-vexed billows whitened into foam, the wild faces of the sea Nereids rose above the glistering swirl, and marvelled at the strange portent. On that day mortals saw the sea-born nymphs with naked limbs, rising breast-high out of the radiant sea. Then Peleus is said to have been set panting with love for Thetis, then Thetis despised not human marriage, then the Father of the Gods confessed that Peleus must be wed to Thetis.

Beautiful and logical, Winckelmann's theory was by far the most convincing yet formulated, and would be reasserted and reworked by several later scholars.

*

If, when you arrived in Rome, you were not important enough, or just not lucky enough, to be able to engage Herr Winckelmann, you might fall into the hands of another famous guide for Roman tourists, James Byres. Byres was a Scot, effectively in exile from his native land, and the fate that brought him to Rome was decided during the revolt of 1745, when Bonnie Prince Charlie, the 'Young Pretender', sought to seize the throne of England. Byres was the next person to gain possession of the Vase, so it could be said that the fate of the Vase was also determined on the bloody battlefield of Culloden.

Patrick Byres, Laird of Tonley, rallied to the standard of rebellion raised by Bonnie Prince Charlie in Glenfinnan in August 1745, and became a major in a Jacobite regiment. He fought at the battle of Prestonpans, a brilliant victory for the Jacobite forces, and marched with them as far south as Derby as they evaded the forces sent to bar their way and threw London into panic. He was part of the retreat when a failure of nerve on the part of the war council lost Charles his golden chance. He was present when the Jacobite army was brought to bay by the Duke of Cumberland, younger son of King George II, in a marshy wasteland near Aberdeen. The Jacobite soldiers were exhausted; they had spent the previous night on an abortive forced march to try to take their enemy by surprise, and more than a thousand of them actually slept through the battle. They had rain and snow blowing in their faces, and were outgunned by Cumberland, who took advantage of the wide open battlefield to decimate the rebels with his artillery before their attack could be brought home (the word to advance failed to get through for some time because messengers kept being killed by the cannon). Finally launched, the wild Highland charge with shield and broadsword (which is perhaps something of a myth – most of the Jacobite soldiers were armed with muskets like their opponents) broke two British regiments, but was halted by a fierce counter-attack. The impetus was lost, and under murderous musket-volleys the whole army disintegrated. In the ensuing rout, 'Butcher' Cumberland's soldiers killed more men than died on the battlefield. The revenge of the house of Hanover was ruthless and barbaric. Many atrocities were committed, including the piling up of wounded Jacobites into heaps to be used for cannon target practice. Prince Charles was hunted through the heather for months, and spent three weeks living in a cave before he could find a ship to take him to refuge in France. Patrick Byres, with the rest, fled for his life.

After Culloden he was hidden by a friend in a castle near to his own lands and then, like his Prince, escaped to the Continent. Patrick had a son, James, who was eleven years old at the time of the 1745 rebellion, and the course of his young life was thus drastically changed by this disastrous conclusion; he went into exile with the rest of the family, was educated in France and brought up in the Catholic religion. So as a young boy James lived through the bloody and dramatic events of 'the '45'. Did he idolise his father and see romance and glory in the failed cause? How bitterly did he feel the exile from his inheritance? He must have identified with the cause, because, like many other Jacobites, his father served with the forces of France in the Royal Scottish Regiment, and we know that when James reached manhood he followed him to the French colours, serving under the Jacobite general Lord Ogilvy. In 1756 he left the army, probably because of a law passed by the British Government designed to confiscate the estates of Jacobites who did not return to Scotland. Although Patrick Byres's lands should have been forfeit after the rebellion, there is a story that, thanks to an administrative sleight of hand performed by a sympathiser, his name never appeared on the list of proscriptions and his possessions escaped confiscation. However, even if the family could retain their possessions, it is clear that Scotland could not be home for James. At the age of twenty-four he went to Rome, which had become the home of a despairing and drunken Prince Charles and the last resting place of the Jacobite cause. Once there, James began to study painting. Eventually it became clear that he did not have the talent to make a successful career as an artist, and he switched to architecture. He did not have the talent to make a successful career of this, either, but it took him the rest of his professional life to discover that fact.

To begin with he showed a moderate amount of promise. After ten

[77]

years in the city he won third prize in a competition run by the
Academy of Saint Luke. His first commission, in 1768, was to design
a house for a fellow countryman, Sir Lawrence Dundas, to be built in
Edinburgh, but the design was rejected. Then the College of
Physicians in Edinburgh asked him to draw up designs for a library; it
was never built. The following year Lord Arundel asked Byres to
design an altar for the chapel in his house at Wardour, and even this
small-scale project came to nothing. In 1770 Sir Watkin
Williams-Wynn commissioned Byres to design a house for him in the
Dee Valley. Once again, this was not taken up. Nor were his designs
for Henham Hall, commissioned by Sir John Rous, nor his temple for
an island on Lord Breadalbane's estate, nor his plans for a house for
the Earl of Charleville. Byres's persistence is admirable, but the
constant rejection must have had an adverse effect on his spirit.
Unable to find success in his chosen field, Byres was forced to resort
to another – antiquities.

While pursuing his studies in Rome, Byres had fallen gradually
under the spell of the ancient remains. He travelled to Etruria, and
made a study of the Etruscan tombs. He published a large volume of
beautiful architectural drawings, *Sepulchral Caverns of Tarquinia*,
Tarquinia being the capital of the Etruscan lands. These highly
detailed drawings give a powerful impression of the spooky
mausoleums, decorated by a vanished people. Byres seems to have
identified to some extent with the Etruscans, sympathising with their
unsuccessful struggle against the dawning power of Ancient Rome,
perhaps seeing in the destruction of Etruscan culture by the Romans
a reflection of the fate of his own nation.

Thus his love of the past and his artistic and architectural training
perfectly equipped him for a career as a guide to visitors on the Grand
Tour, and here he finally found his *métier*. Byres charged twenty
sequins for his course, or thirty for two pupils together. His
reputation as an expert ensured a steady stream of takers. But he does

not seem to have chosen his career out of any love of or even ability for communicating with his clientele. However great his aptitude for the job, however wide his knowledge, it seems Byres hated his chosen profession. He did it for the money, and resented it bitterly – resented the need of the failed artist and architect, the exile from the ancestral lands, to lower himself to earn a living as a tour guide and thereby compromise his status as gentleman. Although his close relationship with his noble and wealthy pupils gave him the ideal opportunity to attract architectural commissions, the constant failure of any of these schemes to achieve success can hardly have reconciled him to the indignity of his position. It is more than likely that he harboured animosity towards his English clients because of the history of political conflict he had lived through; after all, these were the sons of the men who had driven him and his father from their homeland, and murdered his father's friends.

Dr John Moore met Byres Senior in Rome, and recorded the chauvinistic rant he found himself listening to: Loch Lomond was far better than any Italian lake, Campagna looked like a desert compared to the smiling valley of Stirling. From the shortcomings of Italy it was a but a step to those of England: the Thames was a gutter compared to the Firth of Forth, St James's Palace a 'shabby old cloister' beside the glories of Holyrood, and so on. Byres Junior was certainly very learned, and may not have been as crotchety as his die-hard father, but there is no getting over the fact that he was in fact a miserable, foul-tempered pedagogue, as the accounts of his many pupils, in *A Dictionary of British and Irish Travellers in Italy*, attest. 'I am (as you may suppose) up to the ears in Antiquities under the Auspices of Mr Byres,' recorded Thomas Clarke, 'of whose lessons, entre nous, I begin to be rather sick.' Philip Yorke, who visited Rome in the 1770s, gives us a sketch of Byres's methods. Byres had 'no regular system of showing Rome' but determined his agenda according to the weather: 'antiquities and ruins when fine, statues and palaces when wet, and if

it should be a clear day but unpleasantly windy we see pictures.'
Thomas Clarke described him as 'An intelligent man, though a very
disagreeable one'. Thomas Brand mimicked Byres's 'Ayberdeen
Deealect', and was even more forthright: 'A sad, peevish fellow who
would quarrel with his own shadow.' Brand assiduously tried to take
notes 'but he went on at such a rate ... that it was impossible to keep
up with him'. Byres's rival guide Winckelmann thought him a timid
hypochondriac. Charles Long was 'not sorry to have done with a man
who is one of the most irritable I ever met with'.

Dr John Parkinson, who visited Rome in the early 1780s, left a
detailed description of a single day spent under Byres's tutelage, and
just reading it leaves one feeling dazed and footsore. They visited the
Theatre of Marcellus, the Temple of Piety, the Arch of Janus, the
Arch of Septimius Severus, the Cloaca Maxima, the Temple of
Pudicitia, the Temple of Vesta, the Temple of Fortuna Virilis, the
ruins of the Palatine bridge, the House of Crescentius, the Aventine
Hill, the Temple of Juno Regina, the Priory of Malta, and the Pyramid
of Caius Cestius, at the foot of which, presumably, Dr Parkinson
collapsed, begging for mercy. Byres accompanied the tour with a
never-ending flow of information. Dr Parkinson records how their
stop by the Cloaca Maxima tempted Byres from speculation about the
origins of the ancient city, to extravagant deviations and divagations
into such matters as why sirens' feathers became the emblems of the
Muses, and whether the Mediterranean had once been dry land. To
begin with his pupils found this unstoppable flow impressive, but
before long they were most of them wishing he would just shut up.

Perhaps Byres's greatest achievement as a teacher *manqué* was his
baleful effect on Edward Gibbon, a man who possessed so great an
interest in and sympathy for the classical world that he determined to
make it his life's work, and whose *Decline and Fall of the Roman Empire*
is still regarded as the first and greatest work of modern historians.
Gibbon arrived in Rome in October 1764, and the excitement he

describes in his memoirs at this epiphanic experience comes as a telling contrast with Byres's contemptuous familiarity:

> At the distance of twenty-five years I can neither forget nor express the strong emotions which agitated my mind as I first approached and entered the *Eternal City*. After a sleepless night, I trod with lofty step the ruins of the Forum; each memorable spot where Romulus *stood*, or Tully spoke, or Caesar fell, was at once present to my eye; and several days of intoxication were lost or enjoyed before I could descend to a cool and minute investigation.

Unfortunately, he elected to make this under one guide in particular, and he also made the mistake of signing up for a truly epic course of instruction: 'My guide was Mr Byres, a Scottish antiquary of experience and taste. But in the daily labour of 18 weeks the powers of attention were sometimes fatigued.' This then is James Byres's claim to fame: he managed to bore the author of *The Decline and Fall of the Roman Empire* with Roman antiquities.

Fortunately, Byres had another string to his bow, and one that better suited his well-educated taste and vinegary temperament: he also dealt in antiquities. His house was a showroom, stocked with valuable and beautiful objects, arranged with exquisite taste in order to catch and enchant the customer's eye. In the reception rooms of his apartment plaster busts stood on gilt and marble-topped tables. Old Masters, such as Claude Lorraine and Correggio, hung on the walls. His private rooms, on the other hand, were austere, as though symbolising the disassociation this uncomfortable and unhappy man felt between his true identity and the position that fate had thrust on him.

Byres was also more successful in this role than as a teacher. He pulled off some major deals. In 1764 he bought a Poussin from one

Count Solderini, and sold it to Lord Exeter. His biggest coup was the acquisition of Poussin's cycle, the *Seven Sacraments*, which belonged to the Bonapaduli family. Byres sold these paintings to the Duke of Rutland in 1785. There was a significant amount of skulduggery involved in this exchange, because then as now there were regulations restricting the export of artworks, and Byres and his clientele resorted to deception in order to evade them. Byres was keen to remain anonymous, as a surviving note in his hand makes clear: 'It should never be mentioned through whose hands he got them, for my name being mentioned might be attended with the worst consequences to me here, where we live under a despotic government who are more jealous than ever of things going out of Rome.'

The paintings were removed one by one, and replaced by specially commissioned copies. But these pictures were, like the Vase, a customary stop on the Grand Tour. How could Byres now take his charges on a visit to look at copies? According to the contemporary English artist Joshua Reynolds, Byres did not baulk at the necessary deception, combining his role of black-market art-dealer with that of guide and teacher in order to reinforce the fraud. Reynolds claimed that Byres agreed to continue bringing visitors to view the copies, and asserted that they were the original works, thus shoring up their fraudulent title. Reynolds even spitefully speculated that the same trick could be pulled again – another wealthy patron could be duped into buying the copies in the Palazzo Bonapaduli as originals, and more copies put in their place, and so on. There is also some evidence that Byres passed off a modern copy of an antique gem, made by a friend and famous gem-engraver called Giovanni Pichler, as an original on an unsuspecting customer. That the copy was good enough to fool Winckelmann is a tribute to Pichler's talent, but not to Byres's honesty.

So when the Princess of Palestrina, Donna Cornelia

Barberini-Colonna could not pay her gambling debts, it was to Byres that she turned, in the hope of raising some ready cash. Donna Cornelia was a descendant of the Barberini, guardian of the heir to the dwindling family fortune (a boy who had not yet come of age and was in no position to prevent the Princess from squandering his inheritance). Unfortunately her weakness for card-playing had exacerbated the financial crisis in the once proud family. Being a Princess, she had no desire to part with her jewels or her gowns, but one thing, gathering dust on the mantelpiece, she could sell: the Vase. She sold it to Byres in 1780, and it was the 'Barberini Vase' no longer. According to one account the Princess wanted to put onto the market several antiquities from the Barberini collection, including some significant and substantial classical statues. (The 'Barberini Faun', for instance, was a large classical work that depicted a sensual young creature in a state of exotic languor, and was the favourite work of the Marquis de Sade, who described it as a 'sublime statue grecque'. It was eventually sold to Crown Prince Ludwig of Bavaria in 1814.) Unfortunately, the Pope got to hear of the projected sale and forbade the removal from Rome of any of these items. The Vase, however, was small enough to slip through the official net. To Byres, who could spirit away an entire cycle of large oil paintings, a small piece of glassware presented little difficulty.

This transfer marked a new epoch for the Vase; no longer the prize of treasure-seekers, cardinals or popes, it was now in the hands of a dealer, who most appreciated its value professionally, and saw it chiefly as a way to make money. We might say that it passed now into the hands of a truly modern man. Byres was clearly only buying the Vase in order to sell it on; he bought it for about five hundred pounds, expecting to make a profit, and as we shall see his expectations were fully realised.

While the Vase was in his hands, Byres speculated as to how it had been made, and if subsequent attempts to reproduce it are anything to go by, he came close to the truth. Thomas Windus describes the process as follows:

> The glass-maker who formed it for the hands of the sculptor first took on the end of his pipe a mass of the deep blue glass, but before he began to form his vessel he dipped this mass into a pot of white enamel, and thus gave it the form which the sculptor desired, but it is probable that he spoiled several before he succeeded in making one fit for the purpose intended. This being accomplished, the sculptor cut and formed all the figures and ornaments in the white coating, and then cut or ground off all the other parts of the coating, so as to lay bare the deep blue, and make it the surface from which the white figures and ornaments projected. These, in consequence of a small degree of transparency in the white enamel, have an amazing delicacy and beauty in their parts, such as the foliage, and the wings of the flying figure, and the hair.

A few years later, in his mid-fifties, Byres left Rome and returned to Scotland. The political situation had changed, transformed by the cataclysm of the French Revolution, and returning second-generation Jacobites no longer risked decapitation on Tower Hill. Byres could even re-inhabit his ancestral home at Tonley. Byres spent the last thirty years of his life improving and beautifying his estate in Scotland, living to the age of eighty-four. His unhappy heart and his ill temper seem to have been mollified by his long-deferred homecoming. He even, according to a family chronicler, 'cherished affection for a Miss Fraser of Castle Fraser, but something came between them'. Neither of them married, and when Miss Fraser died she left Byres her carriage and her picture, and we can only hope that he was more interested in the subject of the portrait, than in the relative merits of whichever artist produced it.

Ninth Fragment
James Tassie and John Keats

Before Byres sold the Vase, he considered other ways to turn it to his advantage. He asked his engraver friend Giovanni Pichler to make a mould from it. Pichler created a mould of plaster of Paris, and it was divided up into four sections: three for the body of the Vase, and one for the base. Once this delicate operation had been successfully performed Byres could then commission copies from the mould. For this he went to James Tassie.

Tassie is a small but significant figure in the story of the Vase, not just because he was the first person – but by no means the last – to make a three-dimensional copy of it, but because his work and the part the Vase played in it are a prime example of the hold that the Vase, along with other works of antiquity, was beginning to exert over the contemporary imagination.

Tassie was another Scot, born in Glasgow to a working-class family, and apprenticed as a stonemason. But he had talent, and hopes of becoming a sculptor, and managed to get himself into the Glasgow Academy. He then took a job in Dublin, as assistant to Dr Henry Quin, a professor of physics. Quin had a hobby, casting reproductions of engraved gems and precious stones. He and Tassie together invented a medium for reproducing such items, which has been variously described as a 'white enamel paste' and a 'vitreous paste'. It seems to have been made of powdered glass and pigment, which when heated became a workable medium that could be pressed into a mould. But this invention was kept secret, and has subsequently been lost, because what was merely a pastime for the professor became a profession and a thriving business for James Tassie.

Tassie learnt how to reproduce seals, cameos and antique jewels. He brought his new skill to London in the 1760s. He was apparently a shy and diffident man, simple, modest, benevolent. His portrait shows a long, pale face and pale grey eyes, with a sober, earnest expression. He had some difficulty getting started in the turbulent marketplace of the capital, but his reputation soon began to spread, as the quality of his work became apparent. He set up a shop in Great Newport Street, not far from Josiah Wedgwood's showrooms, and indeed he began to supply Wedgwood with moulds for cameos and intaglios, which Wedgwood would then cast in his own ceramic medium.

Tassie's gems became a fashion, then a rage. Jewellers took to setting them in rings, bracelets, and necklaces. A book was compiled – *A Catalogue of Impressions in sulphur of Antiques and Modern Gems from which Pastes are made and sold, by J Tassie, Compton St, 2nd Door from Greek St, Soho*. It described a vast variety of items copied from ancient originals, but now available to the common man for a few shillings. Together, the items were a compendium of ancient history and mythology. An early edition of this catalogue promised that 'The Antiquarian and the Scholar may find gratification of their taste – the Student an assistance to his memory'. It listed over three thousand different entries, under many headings. In the Egyptian section, for instance, were 'Osiris', 'a crocodile' and an 'Egyptian Hawk'. In 'Gods and Goddesses' were 'Saturn', 'Jupiter', 'Juno', 'A Bacchante', '– with a mask', '– sitting with a tiger', '– blowing with pipes', '– dancing like a fury'. Other sub-headings included 'Philosophers, Poets and Orators', 'Kings, Queens and Heroes', 'Roman History' and 'Masks, Chimeras, Vases and Sphinxes'.

By the time Tassie died in 1799, his business was a fixture on the London scene, and was carried on by his nephew, William. There were now more than fifteen thousand items in the catalogue. (Catherine the Great, who was an obsessive collector of gems, placed an order for the entire collection.) William opened a studio in Leicester Square, which became a magnet for artists and poets. The Tassie gems seemed to have a peculiar fascination for the Romantic poets. Byron was a frequent visitor to the shop. Shelley wrote to his friend Peacock, from Italy in 1822, 'I want you to do something for me, that is, to get me two pounds worth of Tassie's gems, in Leicester Square, the prettiest, according to your taste, among them the head of Alexander.'

Three years earlier, in 1819, John Keats had written in a letter to his schoolgirl sister Fanny: 'On looking at your seal I cannot tell whether it is done or not with a Tassi – it seems to me to be paste – As I went through Leicester Square lately I was going to call and buy you some, but not knowing but you might have some I would not run the chance of buying duplicates.' He asks her to let him know if she would like any, and if so, 'whether you would rather have motto ones like that with which I seal this letter: or heads of great Men such as

[87]

Shakespeare, Milton &c – or fancy pieces of Art, such as Fame, Adonis, &c'. A month later he writes again, to let her know that he although he has not forgotten the errand he has not yet been to the Tassie shop. Perhaps this is not surprising, because as well as running errands for his sister he is also, at this time, revolving in his mind the thoughts that will shortly inform the composition of his most famous and successful works, the four great Odes, including his 'Ode on a Grecian Urn'.

> Thou still unravish'd bride of quietness,
> Thou foster-child of silence and slow time.

The subject of Keats's poem is neither Roman, nor a vase. But there is every chance that Keats saw the Vase, and that it contributed, along with many other ancient artworks, to the impressions which inspired the poem. He made a drawing of a Greek vase in the Louvre, known as the Sosibios Vase, which he found in a book by Henry Moses called *A Collection of Antique Vases*. He was also thinking of the Elgin Marbles, newly displayed in the British Museum, and of some of Wedgwood's reproductions of classical motifs. If he visited the British Museum to see the Elgin Marbles – which he almost certainly did – then surely he would have seen the Vase. In any case, his Ode is worth considering because it is the most successful and profound meditation on an ancient work of art in literature, and what it says about the anonymous, composite urn of the title can also be said of the Vase.

Having celebrated the great age of his urn ('foster-child' because the craftsman who made it, its father, is long dead), Keats questions it directly: 'What leaf-fring'd legend haunts about thy shape? ... What men or gods are these? What maidens loth?' Nothing could be more appropriate; these are exactly the questions that scholars have asked, and continue to ask, about the Portland Vase. Keats, perhaps more wisely than they, does not attempt to provide any answers.

Instead, he considers the permanence of the work, its figures frozen for eternity. He could have been addressing these lines directly to figures A and C on the Vase itself:

> Bold lover, never, never canst thou kiss,
> Though winning near the goal – yet, do not grieve;
> She cannot fade, though thou hast not thy bliss,
> For ever wilt thou love, and she be fair!

Love on an urn, then, is better than the real thing.

> More happy love! more happy, happy love!
> For ever warm and still to be enjoy'd,
> For ever panting, and for ever young;
> All breathing human passion far above,

With the power of his own imagination Keats creates the warmth and passion that the urn itself can never supply. He himself, young and unhappy in love, knew what it was to pant, and the contrast between the heat of his verses and the cold, unfeeling urn now undermines his admiration for the work; perhaps it is only a 'Cold Pastoral', sterile and inhuman.

> When old age shall this generation waste,
> Thou shalt remain, in midst of other woe
> Than ours, a friend to man, to whom thou say'st,
> 'Beauty is truth, truth beauty, – that is all
> Ye know on earth, and all ye need to know.'

The final, famous couplet has quotation marks around it; this is not the poet speaking, but the urn itself. Keats, while insisting that the urn is a 'friend', remains ambivalent about its value. It cannot share human suffering, or feel love, and its dictum 'Beauty is truth, truth beauty' is something that a cold and unfeeling piece of perfection might say; it is too simple for the complexities of real, 'breathing' passion, or for the poet himself. Its immortality is undeniable; less than three years after he wrote these lines, Keats himself was dead and buried, in a cemetery in Rome, ending where the Vase began. But Keats is immortal too, and his verses live, while the Vase is at the mercy of any passing vandal with a hangover and a lump of basalt.

*

Byres gave Pichler's mould to Tassie in about 1783. With it Byres gave Tassie permission to make sixty copies, and after that the mould was to be broken, in order, presumably, to preserve the rarity and interest of the copies. At first Tassie only seems to have produced copies of the Vase to order. In 1793, for instance, the Ninth Earl of Burghley ordered one. The procedure for creating a copy was not a particularly speedy one; the finished article was not delivered until May of the following year, along with a bill for ten pounds and sixteen shillings, which was paid by the Tenth Duke, his predecessor having died while waiting for his copy of the Vase. The copies continued to sell slowly, and by the time Tassie himself died, the limit of sixty had not been reached. Half a century later, in 1845, William Tassie had inherited his uncle's stock, and was still advertising a remaining number of copies of the Vase:

> Although these casts have been made more than fifty years, some of them still remain unsold, and may be had of Mr William Tassie, No. 8, Upper Phillimore Place, Kensington, who retains in his own possession the very large Collection of Gems made by his late uncle and himself.

A handful of copies of the Vase by Tassie survive to the present day. Some of them are glazed, but all are monochrome; they do not reproduce the contrasting colours of the original. They are, however, an important record of the way the Vase looked in the eighteenth century, before it was smashed in 1845. The Tassie copies demonstrate that the Vase was not in perfect condition even then. They all faithfully reproduce on the otherwise pristine Vase a crack, semicircular in shape, and about eight inches long, that curves up from the base of the Vase, and down again, running through Figures C, D and E. The Tassie copies supply the only firm evidence that this early crack existed, because it was of course subsequently disguised by later damage.

When did this crack appear? We have no way of knowing whether the damage was done after the Vase made its appearance in the collection of Cardinal del Monte, or long before, in antiquity. But it raises an intriguing possibility – that the Vase suffered a serious accident soon after it was made. The Tassie casts also show that the base disc was not fully inserted into the bottom of the Vase. It was, in fact, slightly too wide, and was cemented onto the rim of the base, instead of fitting snugly inside it. Weathering on the rim of the disc strongly suggests that it was fitted in antiquity. But removal of the base disc in modern times, during restoration, has revealed that the body of the Vase was altered in order to fit the disc.

Under close examination, the rim of the base is revealed as jagged; it has been 'grozed', a process whereby glass can be taken away in tiny bites, using a small metal tool, to alter a piece once it is in its hardened state. The base of the Vase has been so altered, cut down from a larger shape. At some point in antiquity, it would appear that the Vase existed in a different form from that in which it has survived. The base must have extended downwards, probably to a rounded point or knob, and the consensus is that this extension gave the Vase an amphora-style shape, so that it would have required a support to stand upright. Below the existing base of the Vase, another frieze may have run around the narrower lower section, and this has been lost. It is even possible that the alteration took place during the carving of the Vase. Perhaps a crack appeared in the bottom of the Vase during the process of carving, which threatened to spread up the entire body, and drastic action was taken to prevent this in removing the damaged section, and re-shaping the Vase. If this occurred when the carving was well forward, and perhaps years of work had already been invested in the piece, then desperate measures would certainly have been called for.

Here, then, is another mystery: the Vase has not come down to us in its original shape. The grozing is undeniable proof of this, and we have no way of knowing for certain what that shape was. But once this idea is entertained – that what remains is a sort of cut-down version of an original – it is easy to imagine that there is something not quite right about the shape of the Vase. Josiah Wedgwood had an opportunity to examine the Vase itself only a few years after Tassie began to produce his copies. Although he could not see the grozing on the base of the Vase (he would have had to remove the base disc to detect it), and didn't realise the Vase had been cut down from its original shape, Wedgwood the potter had made the study and production of vases ancient and modern his life's work, and felt instinctively that there was something wrong with it. Despite being drawn to the Vase to the point of obsession, he admitted to himself that the shape of the Vase 'is not so elegant as it might be made if the artist had not been possessed of some very good reason for contenting himself with the present form'. Wedgwood speculated as to the reasons for this shortcoming, and found himself making rather lame excuses: perhaps the artist who produced the bas-reliefs had deliberately chosen a less impressive form so as not to distract from his own achievement.

It would seem, then, that misadventure has been part of the Vase's fate from its very conception. We do not know what tears were shed over its original manufacture, or whether some hard-working craftsman's eye or fortune was ruined, or his heart broken, by the fiendishly difficult process of producing the Vase, and all its attendant risks. Tassie and Pichler seem to have survived the experience unscathed, but heartbreak was certainly the lot of those who later attempted to copy the Vase, including Josiah Wedgwood, as we will see.

It is not clear what Byres stood to gain from copying the Vase. Perhaps there was some financial element to his arrangement with Tassie, whereby Tassie paid in order to have access to the mould made by Pichler, in the hope of recouping this expense with the sale of the resulting copies, but it cannot have been a particularly lucrative transaction for Tassie, considering that his nephew still had copies on his hands decades after his uncle's death, and Byres's stipulation that there should be no more than sixty copies would surely have limited his own profit. Perhaps Byres commissioned the mould so that he himself could retain a copy of the Vase for his own enjoyment, because he certainly did not possess the original for long. In a sense, he was never an 'owner' of the Vase, but more a go-between, and he sold it not long after Pichler's mould was successfully produced. The buyer he found was not, as one might expect, a rich and powerful English aristocrat, but an antiquarian like himself, a man who would also, however regretfully, sell the Vase on. Apart, however, from their interest in antiquities and their long residences in Italy, it would be difficult to find two more different characters than the sour, displaced James Byres and a man who made an art of living comfortably, and who became a byword for complaisance as the most famous cuckold in history: Sir William Hamilton.

Tenth Fragment
Sir William Hamilton

William Hamilton was born to a Lady of the Bedchamber who was almost certainly mistress to Frederick, Prince of Wales. This meant that Hamilton was brought up at court, and was, if nothing more, at least a sort of foster-brother to Frederick's son George, the future King George III. So Hamilton was well connected, but he was also a younger son with no fortune to his name, and he would have to make his own way in the world. Like many a younger son he went into the army. He saw the end of the War of the Austrian Succession, and the beginning of the Seven Years War, but played no great part in either; he later confessed to a friend that he suddenly realised that a soldier's life might not be for him when a bullet knocked off the tip of his officer's halberd. It is perhaps surprising that he stayed ten years with the colours, less so that in all this time he rose no higher than captain.

In 1758, in his late twenties, he left the army and sought another traditional recourse of younger sons: he married an heiress, Catherine Barlow, who possessed a small but comfortable fortune, including estates in Pembrokeshire. They settled near Piccadilly, into what appears to have become a genuinely loving relationship, despite the pecuniary motives that underlay it. Hamilton's old playmate was crowned king in 1760, and Hamilton was his equerry. He began to collect pictures, but spent more than he could afford, and ended up selling two collections, one after the other. Catherine suffered from 'an asthma', and in the mini-Ice-Age winter of 1762 her sufferings were severe. Hamilton feared that they would be forced to retire to Pembrokeshire, not a fate he contemplated with any enthusiasm; it was time to ask a favour of his royal patron. In 1763 the post of Envoy to the Kingdom of the Two Sicilies (which at this time included much of southern Italy) became vacant; Hamilton applied for and was given the job. A year later he and Catherine arrived in Naples. Horace Walpole, who now becomes something of a chorus to our story, warned the ambassador at Florence, 'You have a new neighbour coming to you, Mr William Hamilton ... He is picture mad, and will ruin himself in virtu-land.' By 'virtu' he meant all the collectables that Italy offered the connoisseur, pictures and antiquities, and his diagnosis of Hamilton's passion as a collector was barely exaggerated. That passion expressed itself almost immediately, for vases.

Hamilton arrived at a time when the earth around Naples was giving up the most spectacular secrets. The two Roman towns of Pompeii and Herculaneum, buried and preserved by the cataclysmic eruption of Vesuvius in 79 AD, were being excavated for the first time, constantly throwing up all sorts of marvels, from the uncannily well-preserved belongings and bodies of the dead, to wall-paintings and objects that would provide vital evidence for the dating of the Vase. Hamilton observed the digging with great curiosity, and sometimes his reactions revealed a flicker of passions not merely antiquarian, as in this letter to an old friend, Lord Palmerston, in June 1764:

> at the last they have found a Theatre ... In a room just by this building was found a Venus of marble coming out of a Bath & wringing out her wet hair what I thought most remarkable was that all her *tit bits* such as *bubbies mons veneris* &c are double gilt & the gold very well preserved.

The area around Naples had been settled even before the Romans came, by Ancient Greek colonists, and their tombs were now also being opened and ransacked. From these tombs came vases whose decoration preserved the artistry of the Ancient Greeks, some of them made in Athens and Corinth in the fifth century BC, during the heyday of those cities. Almost nowhere else had Greek painting been preserved; indeed, at this time hardly any of the highest Greek art had been discovered or recognised, and now these vases provided glorious examples of an ancient artistry which survived in no other form. Hamilton became obsessed with them. He bought from tomb-robbers and dealers, and he also went in for a little treasure-hunting and tomb-opening himself. Before very long he had amassed a collection of several hundred ancient vases. He was quick to realise the importance of his collection, and arranged to have it catalogued. The first volume came out at the end of 1767: *Collection of Etruscan, Greek and Roman Antiquities from the Cabinet of the Honble. Wm. Hamilton His Britannick Majesty's Envoy Extraordinary at the Court of Naples.* Being himself only a gifted amateur, and conscious that his time in the army had denied him the chance to gain any real scholarly grounding, Hamilton approached Winckelmann to provide accompanying text for the illustrations of his collection.

Hamilton had met Winckelmann in Rome, on a holiday from his duties in Naples. He had hired James Byres as a guide to the antiquities, but fortunately he also called on the services of Winckelmann, with whom, not surprisingly, he got on much better. They developed a high degree of mutual respect: Hamilton for his guide's learning, Winckelmann for his pupil's taste. Winckelmann even seems to have found Hamilton so tolerant and easy-going that he was able to set aside to some degree the mask that concealed his homosexuality. Winckelmann understood the significance of Hamilton's collection, and agreed to supply explanatory notes. He came to visit Naples to see the vases. He took a trip up Vesuvius, which was very active at this time, and picnicked beside the lava, naked in the heat, in the company of a friend, Baron Riedesel, and another antiquarian, 'Baron' d'Hancarville, who was acting as Hamilton's publisher for the vase-volumes. Unfortunately, not long after a viewing of Hamilton's vases Winckelmann was murdered by a piece of rough trade, as we might now say, met on the waterfront in Trieste. Even with this setback, and without Winckelmann's contribution, Hamilton's book had an enormous impact. Josiah Wedgwood, in the process of opening his new factory in the Potteries, began to produce copies of Hamilton's vases from the prints in the first volume. He described them as

truly Greek workmanship, and ornamented chiefly with Grecian subjects, drawn from the purest Fountain of the Arts; it is probable that many of the Figures and Groupes upon them, preserve to us Sketches or Copies of the most celebrated Greek paintings; so that few Monuments of Antiquity better deserve the Attention of the antiquary, of the Connoisseur, and the Artist.

This was the beginning of a relationship between Wedgwood and Hamilton that was to prove highly significant in the history of the Vase.

In 1771, Hamilton and his wife Catherine returned to England on leave. Hamilton brought his vases with him. Horace Walpole viewed them and was suitably impressed. Hamilton needed to sell them in order to recoup the money he had spent on their acquisition and the elaborate publication. But Hamilton was not such a cold-blooded dealer as Byres; he wanted his vases to belong to the nation, and for once the nation did the decent thing. The vases went to the British Museum, and Parliament voted more than eight thousand pounds in payment to Hamilton. After his return to Naples, one of Hamilton's friends, Dr John Elliott, wrote to describe the impact of his collection. The whole country was now mad for vases:

Your collection forms one of the greatest and most admired ornaments of the metropolis, even foreigners come to see it. I have with much satisfaction seen the advantageous manner, in which the inestimable remains of antiquity are arranged. I really think, that the national taste has received a rapid improvement from them; in place of the ponderous dull ornaments we formerly had, we have now the pleasure of seeing new embellishments daily rising up, where every thing is formed in the elegant manner of the Ancients. The Furniture of even the houses is already changed. These improvements are totally owing to that choice collection, which you have set before the publick. In the most ordinary houses ... we see the chimney pieces and cabinets decorated with vases.

Hamilton and Catherine returned to Naples and for another decade Hamilton pursued his interests there as before. Vesuvius was still active, and Hamilton, whose great virtue seems to have been an ability to take an eager interest in whatever was going on around him, became an expert vulcanologist, making dangerous forays to the lip of the crater, observing the phenomena of eruptions from less than a safe distance and writing up his experiences for the Royal Society, who rewarded his efforts with a Fellowship. His marriage seems to have continued a success. His wife certainly loved him. As her health failed in the spring of 1782, she wrote him touching letters:

> I feel my weak, tottering frame sinking & my spirits fail me; my only regret in leaving this world is leaving you; was it not for that I should wish the struggle over. But my heart is so wrapp'd up in you that you are like the soul that animates my body. You never have known half the tender affection I have bourne you because it has never been in my power to prove it to you – forgive this effusion of my heart. I feel myself every day declining.

Catherine's presentiment was entirely correct; she was dying. Did her husband return her love? When she wrote him this letter he was in the process of buying a most expensive piece of 'virtu'; it was not the only thing of beauty he would acquire over the coming months.

Hamilton visited Rome again in the summer of 1782. It is no surprise that he visited James Byres's showroom apartments; Winckelmann had noted that Hamilton was always on the lookout for something to buy, either for pleasure or profit, and here he found something that would satisfy both motives. He saw the Vase, lately removed from the Palazzo Barberini, sitting amongst Byres's collection of busts and paintings. The Vase was, as one might say, in his shop-window, perhaps therefore feeling that it had come down in the world a little. Hamilton described the moment in a subsequent letter to Josiah Wedgwood:

> the superior excellence of this exquisite masterpiece of ancient art struck me so much at first sight, that I eagerly asked, 'Is it yours? Will you sell it?' He answered, 'Yes; but never under

£1000.' 'I will give you a thousand pounds;' and so I did, though God knows it was not very convenient for me at that moment, and the business was concluded in a moment.

Despite the fact that the 'moment' is recollected in tranquillity, Hamilton's hyperbolic language conveys something of the excitement he seems to have felt when he encountered the Vase for the first time. Byres, who must have known his man and seen vase-mad Hamilton as a hot prospect, leads him through the rich and tasteful displays, and casually arrives at the *pièce de résistance*; the mean-tempered, calculating dealer deftly hooked the enthusiastic dilettante, and Hamilton in gentlemanly fashion extravagantly refuses to haggle. But Hamilton was not a Croesus; his limited funds made him an unusual mixture of connoisseur and businessman. To say that 'it was not very convenient for me at that moment' might suggest that like some modern tourist he had merely left his credit card in his hotel room, but it was in fact a wild understatement. The truth is he simply could not afford to pay a thousand pounds; he did not have such a sum of money in any form. Why, then, did he take the plunge? We know that Hamilton was capable of living beyond his means, but this was a serious act of financial recklessness. Did he, as he suggests, just *have* to have it? Or was his overmastering excitement generated by the scent of a fat profit? Events at least bear the latter theory out: before long, Hamilton had sold the Vase on for nearly double what he paid for it. In order to carry out the transaction with Byres, Hamilton gave him a 'bond', at five per cent. Technically, he was not buying the Vase at all, merely borrowing it; if he could not redeem the bond, then eventually it would return to its original owner, with interest.

In his letter to Wedgwood, while extolling the virtues of the Vase, Hamilton made some extravagant claims for its provenance:

Except the Apollo Belvedere, the Niobes, and two or three others of the first-class marbles, I do not believe that there are any monuments of antiquity existing that were executed by so great an artist; and I have no doubt of this being the work of the time of Alexander the Great, and was probably brought out of Asia by Alexander, whose ashes were deposited therein after his death.

Hamilton may have been floating this exotic theory simply in order to raise the status of the Vase, just as Pietro Santo Bartoli had been keen to associate it with the Emperor Alexander Severus. Despite the fact that there had already been some attempt to identify the figures as pertaining to the myth of Alexander's conception (by Jupiter, in the form of a snake, on Olympias), to imagine that the Vase was made in Asia at the time of Alexander was very wide of the mark, and if seriously meant it betrays Hamilton as a very poor scholar. Certainly his publisher d'Hancarville was deeply contemptuous of the existing attempts to identify the figures. Before we embark on the next interpretation of the figures on the Vase, as supplied by d'Hancarville, it is worth reviewing the career of certainly the most bizarre and unconventional antiquarian ever to study and expound on it.

Baron Pierre d'Hancarville was a liar, adventurer, pornographer, and general all-round scoundrel. His title was almost certainly self-awarded (he was the son of a bankrupt French merchant). Like an antiquarian Barry Lyndon, he racketed through the courts of Europe, dazzling his interlocutors with his brilliance and learning:

His penetrating, voracious eyes, his flaring nostrils, his lips which barely touch each other are the outward signs of his longing to see everything; and then, having seen everything, having known everything, he wins you over with his learning and his prolific and imaginative way of speaking.

His relationship with Hamilton is evidence of how tolerant and broad-minded (or how trusting and gullible) the Envoy was. But both men – one by the standards of the age a decent and relatively respectable member of the Establishment, the other an out-and-out rogue – were brought together by their attraction to and sympathy for the past.

D'Hancarville started his career as a captain in the army of a German princeling. He was imprisoned for debt, but rescued by the Duke of Wurttemberg, and was mixed up with him in a major swindle which involved the 'sale' of the island of Corsica. He was arrested for this, but escaped again, this time apparently taking some of the Duke's silver with him. Europe was, and doubtless still is, full of con-men and tricksters of a like description. But d'Hancarville also found the time to publish a philosophical pamphlet which attracted the attention and praise of Voltaire, and he arrived in Italy with a reputation for the brilliance of his learning as well as the elasticity of his morals. Winckelmann warned a fellow antiquarian, 'When you show him your gems, keep a very close look-out to see what he is doing with his hands.'

D'Hancarville lived on credit, and on the run, and surely some rumour of his reputation must have come to Hamilton's ears. But either d'Hancarville's silver tongue persuaded him, or he decided consciously to set aside the bad and see only what suited him – the world-class antiquarian. When Winckelmann was murdered, it was to d'Hancarville that Hamilton turned for help with his great endeavour – the publication of his collection of vases. In a way his trust was well placed. D'Hancarville was not only a brilliant scholar, he was also a book-designer of genius, and under Hamilton's patronage he produced what has been described as one of the most beautiful volumes of all time. When, halfway through the publication of the four volumes, in December 1769, d'Hancarville was forced to flee Naples, Hamilton was ready to take his part: 'He has been sent out of Naples in a very rough manner indeed, so much so that I thought he must have been guilty of some state crime – but his papers are untouched & no reason given for this violence but that it is the will of His Sicilian Majesty.'

In fact, in order to supplement his income, d'Hancarville had decided to do a little publishing on his own account. He had already inserted some rather racy illustrations into Hamilton's volumes. Now he launched a couple of his own, purely pornographic, works, purporting to illustrate the 'private lives of the Caesars', and the 'secret Cult of Roman women'. This venture (which under other circumstances would have drawn no more than an amused smile from the worldly Hamilton) exemplifies d'Hancarville's dual nature. On the one hand, it was a bare-faced attempt to make a bit of money; on the other hand, it was evidence of d'Hancarville's radical and genuinely held beliefs about ancient art. He developed a theory that all ancient art originated in sexuality. That Hamilton knew of and was influenced by this theory was soon to be demonstrated. But meanwhile, his faith in his collaborator was severely tried. D'Hancarville had taken refuge in Florence, and the plates for Hamilton's volumes had gone with him; indeed, he had pawned them in order to satisfy his creditors, and he himself had gone into hiding in a convent. Hamilton had to set off in pursuit, and when he arrived in Florence, he found that d'Hancarville was in prison again. Not surprisingly, it took several years for the last two volumes to be completed, as d'Hancarville's creditors only allowed him to consult the pawned plates one by one, while he wrote a vast and rambling essay to accompany the illustrations.

At the end of the 1770s, d'Hancarville fetched up in London. Here he managed to captivate another English dilettante, Charles Townley. Townley's patronage allowed him to complete the work in which he laid out his theories on ancient artists, and how they drew their inspiration from the initiation rites of the secret religions of the ancients and from sexuality. This work – *Recherches sur l'origine, l'esprit et les progrès des arts de la Grèce* – naturally confirmed his notoriety, but it also provided him with an opportunity to air his own views about the Vase and the meaning of its figures.

First, with a typically arrogant gesture, he takes a sarcastic swipe at all previous theories. Using a simile designed to show off his own classical learning, he compares those who believed any existing explanation to the god Saturn. According to the myth, Saturn habitually ate his children to prevent any of them supplanting him. When Jupiter was born, his mother gave a wrapped bundle to Saturn, who gobbled it down; the bundle contained a stone, and not the baby, but Saturn failed to notice. So to d'Hancarville previous scholars are like Saturn because they will swallow anything. He goes on to concoct a deliberate parody of an interpretation, by pretending that the Vase is a piece of Christian symbolism. Figure C, the kneeling woman with the serpent, must be Eve, and figure A, the young man to whom she holds out her hand, is therefore Adam. Figure D, chin on hand, is the Almighty, in the process of judging and punishing their behaviour. The trees which frame the action are those of the garden of Eden, bearing fig leaves that will come in useful in a moment, and the pillars, being Doric in style, the most ancient of orders, must surely be the gates to the Earthly Paradise. On the other side of the Vase, the female figure with the extinguished torch is the Angel that guarded those gates, and carrying a torch instead of the flaming sword described by Milton in *Paradise Lost*. Therefore, d'Hancarville concludes facetiously, the Vase was made at the time either of Adam or of Oliver Cromwell.

This would be more a more effective piece of satire if d'Hancarville's own interpretation were more strongly reasoned. Unfortunately, his irony rebounds on him, and only reinforces and continues the distinguished record of scholarly obtuseness. D'Hancarville declares that the Vase depicts the myth of Orpheus and

Eurydice. Orpheus is the musician of supernatural power who falls in love with the nymph Eurydice. They are married, but at the ceremony the torch of the marriage-god Hymen smokes instead of burning with a clear flame, and soon after this unlucky omen Eurydice is bitten by a poisonous snake and dies. Orpheus, however, follows her down to Hades, soothing Cerberus, the monstrous guard-dog of the underworld, with his music. Pluto agrees to restore Eurydice to life, and she is allowed to follow Orpheus back to the world above, on condition that he does not turn to look at her, but he cannot resist the temptation, and loses his wife a second time. D'Hancarville declares that figure C, the woman with the serpent, is Eurydice, 'who is constrained to turn her back, but holds out one arm to him, and he endeavours in vain to retain her; the aquatic serpent, from whom she received her mortal wound, is at her side'. So figure A is Orpheus, while D is Pluto, looking on. Nothing violently unreasonable so far, although some sign of a musical instrument would have helped, but it is the other side of the Vase that defeats d'Hancarville. Here he decides to bring in the Heavenly Twins, Castor and Pollux. Why he does this defies explanation; only a moment's inspection would be enough to ascertain that there are no male twins on the Vase. But d'Hancarville gets round this with a suggestion as lunatic as anything that has gone before. Figure E is Pollux, and Castor, though not visible in human form, *is represented by the pillar* that stands beside the figure. Once again the scholar, sensing that his theory does not fit the evidence, adjusts the evidence accordingly.

After his meeting with the Vase, d'Hancarville continued to pursue his rascally career across Europe, espousing the cause of the French Revolution, befriending Thomas Jefferson, and ending his days as a dazzling and mysterious raconteur who could solve any and every problem of artistic interpretation. If his explanation of the Vase is anything to go by, his reputation must have rested more on his bewitching charm than on his powers of reasoning.

*

Little more than a month after Hamilton acquired the Vase he, like Orpheus, lost his wife. Catherine died in August 1782 and Hamilton, who rather prided himself on his stoicism, was surprised at the strength of his grief. After her death, despite all the beauties and distractions of Naples and of his collection he felt very lonely, and the Vase was no consolation. But for him there could be no trip down to the underworld; instead he went home on leave, and took the Vase with him, firmly intending to sell.

Hamilton travelled home overland, staying in Rome and Florence, then heading for Innsbruck, Dresden, and so on to London, but the Vase was sent by ship. Hamilton, after all, had much experience of transporting vases, but he must have organised this one with particular care, watching anxiously as the Vase was packed up in straw, sealed into its case and struck down into the hold. So the Vase left Italian shores and took to sea, almost certainly for the first time in its life, and was carried through the Mediterranean, the Straits of Gibraltar, the Bay of Biscay, and the English Channel. Saved from the terrible jolting of a journey across Europe, it risked instead a watery tomb.

This was no small danger; indeed, Hamilton's next attempt to transport vases by sea was to end in disaster. He sent his last collection home to England in 1799 in order to save it from the inexorable advance of Napoleon's invading army; eight cases of vases, which he described as the cream of his collection, were stowed in the hold of HMS *Colossus*. In a gale off the Isles of Scilly *Colossus* dragged her anchor and ran onto a reef. The crew reached the shore safely, but the ship broke up, pounded to pieces by the terrible surf. There were reports that some of the cases escaped the destruction, and were thrown up on the beach, but only one or two of the vases inside had survived their ordeal unbroken. The commander of a nearby fort, Major Bowen, sent a very strange account of attempts made to salvage the cases, describing how local fishermen took to their boats, and found several of the cases marked with Hamilton's name drifting in the waves. With the gale still blowing and seas still high, the cases were too large and unwieldy to be got into the boats, and the fishermen tried to open them as they floated in the water so that they might retrieve the contents. For what happened next Bowen quotes their account: the fishermen managed to get the cases opened, and saw inside them several large pieces, beautifully painted. However, when they tried to lift the vases out of the water and into their boats, the fishermen found that the vases had somehow softened in the sea and fell apart in their hands, like dough.

Ceramics do not soften in seawater, and this must be a fisherman's tale, perhaps told to account for a failure to recover the cases. But whatever the truth of the matter, only a handful of vases reached Hamilton, who grieved bitterly for his treasures in a letter to his nephew Greville: 'Never in this world will such a collection be made again ... The like were never seen, or ever will be.' The disaster was also a serious blow to his finances, and called forth all his philosophy. But his stoicism was rewarded by the discovery, two years later, that cases sent in another ship contained, not as Hamilton supposed, the dregs of his collection, but nearly all his finest vases, left on the quayside in Naples by mistake, and loaded into this second vessel.

Happily the Vase escaped any such apocryphal melting, or the real threat of a watery grave, and docked safely in the filthy, crowded port of London in the summer of 1783. It had exchanged the blue Italian skies for a northern climate; from now on it would have to endure the damp English air. Once reunited with his prize possession, Hamilton proudly presented the Vase to the Society of Antiquaries, as one of its members recorded in the minutes of the meeting for 11 March 1784:

Sir Wm. Hamilton was pleased to produce, for the Inspection of the Society a Vase singularly curious brought by him from Italy, & purchased there at great Expence. It is called, by way of Excellence and Distinction, the *Barberini Vase,* having been many years in possession of that Noble Family, & considered by them, & all Travellers of Taste and Judgement, as a Cimelium of extraordinary Curiosity and Value.*

Hamilton also made a presentation to another Society – the Society of Dilettanti. This was an altogether less formal body, a dining society founded as a convivial club for gentlemen who had travelled to Italy, and cultivated their taste accordingly. A dilettante being one who cultivates the arts for love rather than for any professional considerations, the Society's minutes declared, 'Whoever shall descend to be serious in earnest thereby deviating from the Originall constitutional sense and spirit of the Society, shall be severely reprimanded.' The Vase, it appeared, was not the only curiosity in Hamilton's cargo. He had something else to show the Society of Dilettanti: a collection of 'votive offerings'.

Shortly before he acquired the Vase, Hamilton had learned of another, rather more bizarre connection with the ancient world, which was to be found in the remote town of Isernia. This was a church festival dedicated ostensibly to Saint Cosimo. Just as Hamilton formulated the desire to attend the festival, it was suppressed by the Bishop, and he had to base his account on second-hand sources. But he duly presented it to the Society, and another member wrote up the findings and published them, together with plates of illustrations of the offerings themselves.

According to Hamilton's account in a letter to Sir Joseph Banks, every year on the saint's day (27 September) local women would

* A cimelium, according to the *Oxford English Dictionary*, is a treasure or thing 'laid up in store as valuable'.

come into town and purchase votive offerings: 'In the city, and at the fair, ex-voti of wax, representing the male parts of generation, of various dimensions, are publickly offered to sale.' These offerings, referred to euphemistically as the Saint's 'Great toe', were then taken by the women to the church. 'In the vestibule are two tables, at each of which one of the canons of the church presides.' A large basin for the reception of different offerings is set up here, then 'The vows are chiefly presented by the female sex.' Hamilton's text describes how his source 'told me also, that he heard a woman say, at the time she presented a vow "Cosimo, let it be like this" ... The vow is never presented without being accompanied by a piece of money, and is always kissed by the devotee at the moment of presentation.' (If the appearance of the wax objects was anything to go by, 'like this' meant large and in a state of tumescence.) At the altar, the 'oil of Saint Cosimo' was offered to the male congregation: 'Those who have an infirmity in any of their members, present themselves at the great altar, and uncover the member affected; and the reverend canon anoints it.'

This was all very interesting, and no doubt tickled the Dilettanti. One wrote to Hamilton, 'I shall like to see our matrons handling the great toe of Saint Cosimo in the British Museum. I wish you would send me one for mine.' But there was a serious point to the research; Hamilton believed that he had detected the survival of a pagan rite, seemingly derived from the worship of the phallic god Priapus. He had discovered a connection to the Ancient Roman world, something still living, every bit as informative as a silent, inanimate Vase. Hamilton's collaborator, who published *An Account of the Remains of the Worship of Priapus*, certainly thought it worthy of serious study, and added a long essay on the veneration of Priapus to Hamilton's account and the drawings of the offerings. But once the book was in print, he and the rest of the Society experienced an attack of nerves; they grew apprehensive of the offence the images might cause, and tried to restrict the circulation of the copies.

Hamilton may also have shown the Society his Vase in order to attract likely customers. He desperately needed to sell it – not only in order to pay off the bond he had given to James Byres, but also to make a profit on the transaction, with which he could pay off some of his many other debts. Fortunately, the right customer almost dropped into his lap. In London, now a lonely widower, he took up with his young niece, Mary Hamilton. Hamilton's brother Charles was dead; Mary, his daughter, was in her twenties, attractive and vivacious, and Hamilton enjoyed going about with her, in an avuncular fashion. By the happiest of accidents, Mary had developed friendly ties with the Duchess of Portland, and as a customer for the Vase the Duchess was the most likely candidate Hamilton could hope to find. She was extremely wealthy, and spent a sizeable proportion of her vast fortune on collecting curiosities. Horace Walpole characterised her as 'a simple woman, but perfectly sober, and only interested in *empty* vases'. Through Mary, engineering an invitation to the Duchess's country seat at Bulstrode Park was easy enough, and so began a comedy of intrigue and manoeuvring.

*

The first scene of this comedy opened at Bulstrode Park. On a brief visit, accompanied by his niece, Hamilton made his entrance as an exotic guest, deeply tanned from his sojourn under a foreign sun, perhaps even singed by his daring encounters with Vesuvius, and all the more interesting as being in mourning for his poor dead wife. In his conversation he mentioned the Vase as one item in a stream of fascinating details and anecdotes, just enough to pique the Duchess's interest.

The second scene shifted the action to Whitehall. Hamilton and

Mary visited the Duchess again, this time at her London residence. He was shown her private museum of natural and artificial curiosities. No explicit mention was made of how well the Vase would sit as the centrepiece or crowning glory of this collection, but doubtless the implication hung heavy in the air. The Duchess remarked casually that she would *quite like* to see the Vase.

The third scene took place at Hamilton's lodgings. Mary recorded the action of this scene in her diary, beginning with the entrance of the Duchess's old friend and confidante, Mrs Delany: 'Mrs Delany and the Duchess came to me, and we went to my uncle, Sir William, at his hotel in King Street. The Duchess saw the fine vase, etc, etc, stayed till half past three o'clock. The pain in my face continued very bad' (the cold weather had inflamed poor Mary's neuralgia). So Mrs Delany and the Duchess got their first look at the Vase, but in a thank-you note sent on New Year's Day 1784, Mrs Delany played it down. The Duchess herself was a martyr to neuralgia, and sometimes swaddled herself in six or seven cloaks and coats, but for Mrs Delany it would seem Mary's distressing condition took precedence; the Vase is only mentioned in parenthesis. 'Tell me how you do today my dear Miss Hamilton. I hope your goodness to me yesterday did not add to your teazing complaint. The calm, delightful society of yesterday, not forgetting the *vase*, did me more good than freezing fingers can express. I am impatient for Saturday. Ever yours, M. D.'

In the fourth scene of the comedy the action reached its crisis. Mary's diary again:

Went to Mrs Delany's home in Saint James's Place. She took me aside to say she had a *secret message* for me from the Duchess. Then, under the cover of getting me to look for a book she took me to her bedroom and told me what the Duchess wanted me to do, viz – to purchase the vase of my uncle. Immediately sent a note to him, but learnt that he was not at home, because, quite by chance he had decided to call on Mrs Delany and was *at that moment* announced! I took him down to the parlour under pretence of showing him the pictures, and then told him what the Duchess wished about the vase. When we came upstairs again they talked upon the subject. My uncle brought me home at ten o'clock. He told me he would think upon what the Duchess had said.

The next scene was effectively a soliloquy. Hamilton, at his hotel, analysed in a letter to Mary the events of the night before, and wrestled with the problem of how best to clinch the deal and what sum to name. He presented his tactics to his go-between (the asides have been interpolated):

My Dear Niece. I have been thinking much upon what passed last night and now I will open my mind freely to you on the subject, and you may make use of what I write as far as you think proper, and with your usual prudence. (*Well done so far, now I am relying on you to pass this on to the Duchess.*) In first place, there is something in the act of selling that gives a disagreeable sensation, particularly when the value of the objects for sale can only be ascertained by what the French call *prix d'affection*. (*Of course I don't want to sell the Vase at all. I am a gentleman, not a low, filthy dealer, and I'd rather hang on to it. After all, it's priceless, isn't it?*) However, as the first proposal did not come from me, but from the Duchess, I shall at once make what I think a reasonable offer to her Grace. (*But of course if she were to offer me a suitably enormous sum of money, I might be induced to part with this great treasure, just out of politeness, really.*)
I am very sure I could directly get two thousand pounds from the Empress of Russia, but I cannot bear the thought of its

going out of England now it is once safe here, for there is not such a monument to antiquity in the world.

Scene Six was the climactic meeting; Mary went to see the Duchess in Whitehall. She dutifully and tactfully passed on her uncle's position, his courteous willingness to sell, his ruthless play for a colossal price. Hamilton's threat to take the Vase to Catherine the Great was a real one: the Empress was herself a voracious collector with resources far beyond even the Duchess's, and he would later attempt to sell her his Correggio. Mary wrote, 'To Mrs Delany's again, to meet the Duchess. She and I went into Mrs Delany's bedroom and I told her what Sir William had said about the *Vase*.' Hamilton had judged his victim well. The Duchess *was* as rich as Croesus; she was besotted with the Vase and she did not baulk at the amount.

The final scene is provided, once again, by entries in Mary's diary: 'Went to the Duchess of Portland's. My uncle came at the same time, and she shewed him many of her fine things. He stayed till half past three; they talked over and settled the affair of the vase.' In other words, they haggled. But not much; Hamilton accepted eighteen hundred pounds, and thus made himself eight hundred pounds clear profit, less whatever interest was owing on the bond he had given James Byres. The Vase was the Barberini Vase no longer. From now on it would be the Portland Vase.

*

While Hamilton was playing out this comedy with his niece and the Duchess, he was also spending some time with his nephew, Charles Greville. The childless Hamilton was happy to make time for both niece and nephew; he had a good relationship with Greville, who, like himself, was a younger son required to make his own way. In this way

1. The Vase: Side I

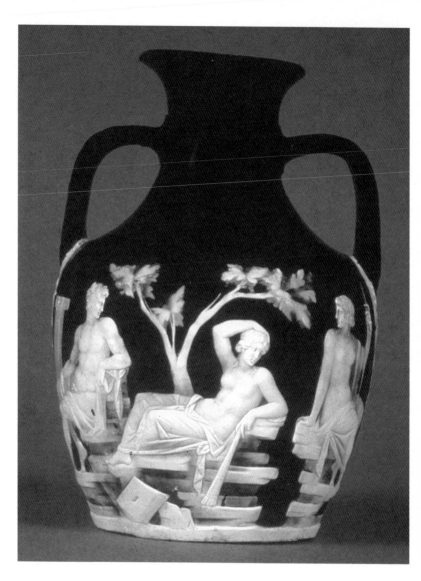

2. The Vase: Side II

3a. Fragments of the Vase. Watercolour by T. Hosmer Shepherd, 1845

3b. Fragments of the Vase during restoration by Axtell. Photograph, 1948

A   B   C   D

E   F   G

4. Line drawing of the figures on the Vase

5. Base Disc of the Vase

Ἔρωτος

Ἔρωτος δ᾽ ὅτι Ἰδαίη, ἢ ἐπὶ νῆός ἐστιν Ἀχαιῶν.

6. The Vase : Side I. Engraving by William Blake, 1791

7. The Vase: Handle

8. Frontispiece to catalogue of the sale of the Portland Museum.
Engraving by Charles Grignon, 1786

he met Greville's teenage mistress, Emily Hart, and was smitten by her great beauty and charm. He arranged for Romney to paint her portrait, and then decided that this was not enough: she must sit for Sir Joshua Reynolds too. His attentions were so marked that Mary began to gossip, particularly with Reynolds's niece, who, as she confided to her diary, 'told me that my uncle William had been often at Sir J Reynolds lately; that he escorted my Cousin Chs Greville's Mistress, in a *Hackney Coach*, & that her Uncle was painting this Woman's picture for him to take to Naples. I shall make use of this intelligence to have some entertainment in *plaguing Sir William.*'

When Hamilton's leave ended and he returned to Naples, he found, naturally enough, that he was lonely without his wife. Greville, who had perhaps already broached the subject before his uncle left, wrote to suggest a deal every bit as delicate as the sale of the Vase. Just like Hamilton before him, Greville needed to marry well in order to secure a living. Two things stood in the way: first, he must dispose of his young and beautiful mistress; secondly, he must acquire some financial standing that would render him acceptable to eligible young ladies in the marriage market. He proposed to kill two birds with one stone. Hamilton could have the lovely Emma, and by way of gratitude could officially make Greville his heir. This proposal was put with remarkable candour; Greville went so far as to describe Emma as a 'modern piece of Virtu' – as it were the living counterpart of the Vase, and a fitting replacement for the finest object in his uncle's collection. In a way his description would prove more accurate than he could have guessed, and by degrees Hamilton acceded to his request. He had doubts – the girl was young enough almost to be his granddaughter – and he took account of a fact that Greville seemed able to ignore: Emma was in love with Greville, and felt that she belonged to him. But in the spring of 1786 Emma was packed off to Naples, ostensibly for a holiday. Hamilton made no secret of his admiration for her, as she tells Greville in the first letter she sends home: 'He ... is constantly by me, looking in my face. He does nothing all day but look at me and sigh. I can't stir a hand, leg or foot; but he is marking as graceful and fine.' From the first, however far it went subsequently, Hamilton's relationship to his young visitor was based on the simple pleasure of looking at her.

Friends and spectators jumped to amused conclusions, and in his letters James Byres made the same vase-analogy as Greville: 'Our friend Sir William is well. He has lately got a piece of modernity from England, which I am afraid will fatigue and exhaust him more than all the volcanoes and antiquities in the Kingdom of Naples.' But things were not quite so straightforward. When it became clear to Emma that Greville had abandoned her, and that she was to stay with the uncle, at first she was heartbroken, and scribbled piteous notes to her betrayer: 'I do try to make myself as agreeable as I can to him. But I belong to you, Greville, and to you only will I belong, and nobody shall be your heir apparent.'*

Hamilton was wise enough not to press her. Over several months he showed her off to the admiring Neapolitans, made sure she enjoyed herself and continually commissioned artists to capture her beauty in paintings, statues, carved gems and snuff-boxes. However far she had come, Emma had certainly begun in life as a common prostitute, and surely knew which way the cold winds of the world blew. Besides, Hamilton was a decent man, kind and loving, certainly more so than his selfish, calculating nephew. By Christmas she had capitulated, and lay back to enjoy Hamilton's adoration, which still more than anything else seemed to involve making copies of his beautiful piece of 'virtu'. His unblushing celebration of her charms made even Emma coy:

those beautys that only you can see shall not be exposed to the common eyes of all, and wile you can even more see the

---

* The spelling of this note was at some point corrected: Emma's was less conventional.

originals, others may gess at them, for the are sacred to all but you, and I wish the wos better for your sake.

She became a permanent fixture in his exquisite Neapolitan lodgings, and she made Hamilton a happy man. He began to collect vases again, and a painter friend saw him one day, coming away from court in his full regalia, lugging along a basketful, having commandeered a street urchin to assist with the other handle. Artists were still queuing to immortalise Emma, but Hamilton hit on an even better way to display her 'beautys'. He discovered in her a talent for acting, specifically the ability to strike attitudes. She could hold a pose, be 'in character'. Perhaps it began as a bedroom game, or when she sat to Romney and Reynolds as 'a Bacchante', or 'Circe', but it quickly grew into something more theatrical. Hamilton taught or encouraged her to present in her poses characters from ancient mythology, to bring to life the figures on his vases. He had a black box constructed which was to be the frame in which she stood, had dresses made for her that imitated the robes of the ancients, and experimented with lighting effects. As Emma's skills became more apparent, however, the act changed, becoming more fluid. Like an impressionist or a mime, Emma began to build up a repertoire of different character-poses, through which she could run one after another. By chance one of the great literary figures of the age, Goethe, visited Naples at this time, saw her private performance and jotted down a description of it:

She is very handsome, and of a beautiful figure. The old knight has had made for her a Greek costume, which becomes her extremely. Dressed in this, and letting her hair loose, and taking a couple of shawls, she exhibits every possible variety of posture, expression and look, so that at the last the spectator almost fancies it is a dream. Standing, sitting, lying down, grave or sad, playful, exulting, repentant, wanton, menacing, anxious, all mental states follow rapidly one after another. With wonderful taste she suits the folding of her shawl to each expression. The old knight holds the light for her, and enters into the celebration with his whole soul. He thinks he can discern in her a resemblance to all the most famous statues of antiquity.

Hamilton had the best of both worlds; conceiving a passion for the beautiful, classical forms that decorated his vases, he contrived like Pygmalion to animate these frozen figures, to metamorphose them into warm and yielding flesh and satisfy his passions both aesthetic and sexual in the worship of his lovely young Muse. He had brought the Vase to life.

Despite the vast differences in age and social status, he married Emma in 1791, but his idyll, of course, did not last. War and revolution swept it away. By the end of the decade he had been forced out of Naples by the advancing armies of the French Revolution; his health was failing, his debts were mounting, his second collection of vases was lost in the shipwreck, and his wife was conducting a very public affair with the greatest British celebrity of the time – Nelson, the Hero of the Nile. Emma's infatuation with Nelson was notorious, and she herself began to succumb to obesity. All three became, in the eyes of the world, figures of fun, Nelson's victories notwithstanding. Stoical to the last, Hamilton gracefully accepted his wife's infatuation, and lived with apparent contentment in a *ménage à trois*, dying two years before Nelson was killed at the moment of victory at Trafalgar. Hamilton had an admirable philosophy, and he certainly needed it towards the end of his life. He drew inspiration from his study of the classical world, from his vases, and even from the Vase itself:

My study of antiquities, has kept me in common thought of the perpetual fluctuation of every thing. The whole art is, really, to live all the *days* of our life; and not, with anxious care, disturb the sweetest hour that life affords – which is, the present! Admire the Creator, all his works, to us incomprehensible; and do all the good you can upon this earth; and take the chance of eternity, without dismay.

Meanwhile the Vase, seemingly immune to the 'perpetual fluctuation' of every other thing in the universe, had disappeared into the collection of the Duchess of Portland.

Eleventh Fragment
The Duchess and Mrs Delany

Horace Walpole could stand as the patron saint of this work; he was all for tracing and recording the history of objects. He knew Sir William Hamilton, and was friend and adviser to the Duchess of Portland. His letters provide us with an invaluable commentary on the career of the Vase during the second half of the eighteenth century. Walpole was quite literally a man of letters; he decided when he was still a precocious teenager that he would make his bid for literary fame through his correspondence. He was the son of a Prime Minister, Sir Robert Walpole, who virtually invented the job and used it not only to dominate the English political scene during the reign of George II, but also to enrich himself unashamedly. So Horace Walpole had money, and connections, but he was still an outsider, perhaps by temperament, and certainly because of his homosexuality. With such resources and detachment, Walpole became a waspish, brilliant observer and recorder of his contemporaries' foibles. Moreover, he cultivated a taste for antiquities and curiosities of all sorts, with which he stocked his greatest curiosity of all, his Gothic villa at Strawberry Hill. It has been said that Walpole revolutionised the taste of the entire nation with this folly, a fantasy concoction of monastic vaults and stained glass, but all on a cosy, domestic scale. Walpole invented a literary genre to complement his architectural trend-setting; in the summer of 1767 he wrote *The Castle of Otranto*, the first Gothic novel, an absurd but strangely compelling mix of the sensational and the supernatural, involving secret passageways, mad monks, abducted heroines and a generally preposterous plot. It spoke to the suppressed urges of the civilised mind, spawned a whole industry of imitators and has never been out of print since.

Walpole made the Grand Tour; his dog it was that was eaten during his crossing of the Alps (much to his distress; he was passionately fond of his little dogs). Once recovered from the shock of his pet's demise he was too busy chasing the other object of his affections, the Ninth Earl of Lincoln, to pay much attention to the antiquities in Rome, but he did acquire a bust of Vespasian, for which he paid twenty-two pounds at Cardinal Ottoboni's sale, and a medal of Alexander Severus. But his tastes were, to say the least, eclectic, and over the years he filled Strawberry Hill with a grotesque melange of objects: curios and valuable paintings, keepsakes and souvenirs, knick-knacks and gewgaws. Visitors were led round four at a time (tickets were free but had to be pre-booked), and they tiptoed about so as not to disturb the author at his desk, admiring his possessions in their unique setting – a lock of hair belonging to Edward IV, a pair of Ancient Roman earrings, a phallic object or two, a silver tea-kettle, contemporary works by Anne Damer, the lesbian sculptress, and by the notorious divorcee Lady Diana Beauclerc, from whom Walpole had commissioned a series of 'soot paintings' (watercolour and charcoal) to illustrate his erotic drama *The Mysterious Mother*. These paintings and the manuscript of the play (which dealt with the theme of incest) were hidden together in a tower, screened by a curtain, and only revealed to a few special guests.

Walpole made a catalogue of his collection. He feared that some might regard the cataloguing of one's own works as rather self-regarding behaviour, and felt the need to defend his actions; those who came after him and wished to buy or sell these objects, he argued in a letter, would greatly benefit from a knowledge of their history and provenance. Each individual history operated like a family tree or a bloodline:

> Such well-attested descent is the genealogy of the objects of virtu – not so noble as those of the peerage, but on a par with those of race-horses. In all three, especially the pedigrees of peers and rarities, the line is often continued by many insignificant names.

But when he wrote this Walpole could hardly have been thinking of his friend Margaret, Duchess of Portland. The new owner of the Vase could not be said to have an insignificant name, particularly as she passed it on to the Vase itself. Walpole himself generously assisted at the enlargement of her collection, of which the Portland Vase was to become the centrepiece. He wrote to a friend in the 1750s: 'My evening yesterday was employed – how wisely do you think? In what grave occupation! In bawding for the Duchess of Portland, to procure her a scarlet spider from Admiral Boscawen.'

Margaret Cavendish Holles-Harley had been born not so much with a silver as with a gold or even platinum spoon in her mouth. She was the daughter of the Earl of Oxford, and on the death of her parents inherited the family fortune, which included Welbeck Abbey and an income of twelve thousand pounds a year. So she was already an heiress when she married the rich and handsome Second Duke of Portland in July 1734, and the union of their fortunes made them colossally wealthy.

The Duke himself was kindly, but retiring. He was a Fellow of the Royal Society and a Knight of the Garter, but he took no part in politics, or in anything else except family life. He was a loving husband who sired six children, and was beside himself with grief and worry when four of them went down with smallpox (all survived). After her marriage Margaret referred to him as her 'Sweet William', and confided to a friend, 'I wish you knew more of the flower, for I am sure you would be delighted by it.' The flower reference is highly indicative of the Duchess's interests; indeed, flowers seem to loom larger in her life than does the Duke himself.

Margaret also enjoyed the life of gilded privilege and pleasure, but within the confines of her palatial houses she seems to have been altogether more active. As an anxious mother who had to see her children through all their illnesses, she became something of an amateur physician, and developed a cure for whooping cough which involved rubbing the spine with rum. She was susceptible to the cold, and got into the habit of dining in a cloak and hood. She was also vivacious and witty; indeed, her friend Mrs Delany sometimes described her as 'provokingly so'. All her friends and acquaintances were given nicknames: 'Pipkin', 'Mrs Sullen', 'Long Nose', 'Wild Beast', and 'the Quilted Petticoat'. She liked men of ability, and they seemed to return the liking. All sorts answered her invitations: explorers, artists and men of letters. She lionised the actor Garrick, and the poet and clergyman Edward Young, author of 'Night Thoughts', a religious poem highly popular at the time. She also had letters from no less a name than the French philosopher Rousseau, who came to stay with her once on a visit to England and kept up a correspondence with his hostess.

The Duchess spent most of her time at her husband's country seat, Bulstrode Park, which she took pains to beautify. She spent time and money on the gardens at Bulstrode, and stocked a menagerie of rare and unusual creatures. She was intensely interested in botany and commissioned the painter Georg Ehret, now considered to be one of the finest botanical artists, to paint more than three hundred pictures of exotic flowers. The Reverend John Lightfoot, a highly distinguished botanist, was retained as family chaplain, and set to work cataloguing the Duchess's rarities. Her patronage of botanists resulted in the naming of a shrub growing in the foothills of the mountains of Jamaica as *Portlandia Grandiflora*. She invited Sir Joseph Banks to Bulstrode soon after that famous scientist had returned from his voyage with Captain Cook.

As a woman of leisure the Duchess also pursued several more or less pointless hobbies, one being 'turning', the shaping of pieces of wood, ivory and jet on a lathe. Her confidante, Mrs Delany, in a similar spirit designed decorations from seashells. She developed her skills in painting cornices to resemble carving, and then was given the task of designing and decorating an entire grotto in the grounds of Bulstrode. But it would be a mistake to view these two women's pastimes as merely trivial, domestic, and amateurish. They both harboured grander passions – the Duchess for curiosities, and Mrs Delany for the art of collage. The Duchess's passion led her, eventually, to the Vase, but the end of Mrs Delany's endeavours is in its way equally remarkable, and the results are, like the Vase, now visible in the British Museum.

Mrs Mary Delany was a daughter of the aristocracy, who, against the wishes of her family, married a clergyman of comparatively modest means, and lived happily with him near Dublin. Hogarth taught her painting, she showed great skill with the needle, and as a child she developed a love of collages. Though childless, she had a long and happy married life, and when her husband died, she went to stay at Bulstrode with her friend the Duchess. She was sixty-nine years old, the Duchess in her mid-fifties; they were both now widows.

During the 1760s, Mrs Delany enjoyed a comfortable and companionable existence with her Duchess. They liked to wander the park at Bulstrode with food for the animals and the peacocks, a sketchbook tucked under the arm, and an eye out for good botanical specimens. Above all, they indulged their love of flowers, and for Mrs Delany, the clergyman's widow, this was no mere distraction. The beauties of Bulstrode took on a moral importance, as she wrote:

> Surely an application to natural beauties must enlarge the mind? Can we view the wonderful texture of every leaf and flower, the dazzling and varied plumage of the birds, the glowing colours of flies &c., and their infinite variety, without saying, *'wonderful and marvellous art thou in all thy works!'* And this house, with all belonging to it, is a *noble school* for contemplations!

In 1772, at the age of seventy-three, Mrs Delany started something new; she wrote to her niece, Mary, 'I have invented a new way of imitating flowers, I'll send you next time I write one for a sample.' She later recounted how, one morning, she was sitting in her bedroom at Bulstrode when she noticed the similarity in colour between the petals of a geranium in the room and a piece of coloured paper that lay on the table. On a 'whim of my own fancy', she picked up her scissors, cut out shapes of petals, found other colours for the leaves and stalk of the plant, and constructed a picture of the plant in collage. This essay was greeted with enthusiasm by the Duchess, and Mrs Delany began to wield her scissors in earnest. She was inventing her own art form – the creation of flower pictures by collage. She may have been intending merely to imitate pressed flowers, but she went much further. She had already spent decades practising embroidery, and in particular the embroidery of flowers. She had spent hours in the company of the Duchess, listening to her interrogate her botanical visitors, and quietly absorbing a great deal of knowledge. She had developed extraordinary skill with scissors; she could cut silhouettes and had a sharp eye for detail. She had already made pictures of birds from cut paper, with astonishingly intricate work on the feathers, as many as eighty-six cuts to an inch of paper. After a lifetime of preparation, it is simply remarkable that in her seventies she still retained the dexterity and unimpaired eyesight that enabled her to create her collages.

They are incredibly detailed and extremely beautiful. The pictures have to be seen in the flesh to be properly believed; even when looking at sumptuous colour illustrations it is almost impossible to conquer the impression that one is looking at a painting, and not a collage. In fact, to begin with, Mrs Delany did apply shading and other detailing to her collages with watercolour. But as she refined her methods, she abandoned this technique, and used only strips and shapes of paper, hundreds for each picture. The petal of a rose, for instance, would be represented by many different pieces of paper, each shape denoting a change in shade as the light fell across the folded surface of the bloom. In the same way the stems and buds of the flowers were built up of several strips of paper of different shades, again to create the effects of the play of light and of three-dimensional form. Her 'White Flowered Acacia' has 584 tiny leaves on its delicate spray, and 120 stamens. She used coloured paper imported all the way from China, or sometimes dyed the paper herself to the desired shade. She designed her works like professional botanical illustrations, the specimen displayed in splendid isolation on a black background, with all its elements shown off to their best advantage.

Close to, the work reveals an astonishing complexity and skill: step back, and the illusion is complete.

Some regarded Mrs Delany's work as merely the amusement of an old and idle woman. She herself played down her 'Paper Mosaicks': 'I can't boast of any useful employments,' she wrote to her niece, 'only such as keep me from being a burthen to my friends, and banish the spleen.' But she had admirers. King George III and his Queen were frequent visitors to Bulstrode (indeed, the King had the disconcerting habit of strolling unannounced into the sitting room), and they at least honoured her efforts, as she recounted proudly in a letter to her niece:

> The King asked me if I had added to my book of flowers, and desiring he might see it. It was placed on a table before the Queen, who was attended by the Princess Royal and the rest of ye ladies, the King standing and looking over them. I kept my distance, till the Queen called me to answer some question about a flower, when I came; and the King brought a chair and set it at the table, opposite to the Queen, and graciously took me by the hand and seated me in it, an honour I could not receive without some confusion and hesitation: 'Sit down, sit down,' said her Majesty, 'it is not everybody has a chair brought them by a king.'

The King and Queen became good friends of Mrs Delany, and when she reached her eighties, and her dear Duchess died and her keen eyesight began to fail at last, they housed her and looked after her at Windsor. Mrs Delany's flower pictures are now kept and displayed by the British Museum, and regarded, like the Vase, as among its treasures. So much discernment, such an artist's eye, were brought to bear on the Vase when Mrs Delany carefully took it up in her mittened hands and held it close to examine it, in William Hamilton's hotel room in King Street.

*

The Duchess inherited her passion for collecting from her father. He also bequeathed to her his cabinet of curiosities, which formed the nucleus for her own collection. This famous piece of furniture, made of ebony and decorated by the artist Polemberg, was known as the 'Ten-thousand-pound Cabinet', because of the supposed value of the precious rarities it contained. These included a dagger once belonging to Henry VIII, set with 'jacinths' (gemstones like sapphires, yellow or blue), an emerald seal belonging to Charles II, and an antique vase of agate decorated with a relief of ram's heads. To this the Duchess added another curiosity inherited from her husband's family: a pearl earring worn by Charles I at his execution. This had been given by William III to her husband's grandfather, the Earl of Portland, with whom, as we shall see, King William was more than just good friends.

The Duchess, botanist and menagerie owner, was as interested in rarities of natural history as in antiquity. The catalogue to her collection lists 'Shells, Corals, Petrifactions, Spars, Ores and Chrystals', 'Fishes and parts of ditto', 'English Insects' and 'Exotic Insects'. Walpole, in an account written after her death, describes how her passions developed as her collection swelled inexorably from one ebony cabinet to fill an entire private museum: 'At first her Taste was chiefly confined to Shells, Japan & old China, particularly of the blue & white with a brown Edge, of which last She formed a large Closet at Bulstrode; but contenting herself with one specimen of every pattern She could get, it was a collection of odd pieces.' Then the Duchess inherited her mother's substantial income. Part of this she spent on her flower garden and menagerie at Bulstrode, but the rest went in indulging her taste for Virtu, sparing no expense to gratify it for about thirty years, her own purchases costing her not less than threescore thousand pounds ... the Duchess began to buy pictures, which She did not understand, & there & in other instances paid extravagantly, as well as for other articles to her taste. Latterly she went deeply into natural history, & Her collection in that Walk was supposed to have cost her fifteen thousand pounds.

Walpole then describes how, in the 1780s, 'She checked her purchases; but some months before her Death she was tempted by the celebrated Barberini Vase.'

She closed her bargain with William Hamilton in February 1784, but it was several months before she took delivery. Hamilton wanted a memento of the Vase, and commissioned engravings of it. Cipriani made drawings of the Vase, and Bartolozzi engraved the plates. These two Italian artists lived together in Golden Square, and there the Vase stayed for some time while the work went on. The drawings were completed in July, while Hamilton was away in Scotland, and in his absence Cipriani delivered them to Mary, as she records in her diary entry for 13 July:

At 12 o'clock Cipriani and another man brought my Uncle's fine Vase, to deposit in my care. He shewed me the Drawings he had made from it which are indeed inimitably executed ... As soon as he left me I sent for a person to make a Box to contain this precious work of Art.

So the Vase joined and took pride of place in the exotic jumble of the Duchess's growing cabinet of curiosities. Her museum was a very private affair, as indeed was the transaction between Hamilton and the Duchess. No word of the purchase got out to the world at large.

According to Horace Walpole, not privy to the secret, the Vase had 'disappeared with so much mystery'. Only the Duchess and her closest circle could enjoy it as it sat, in pride of place, amongst her collection, beside another altogether less distinguished vase of agate, and Henry VIII's jewel-encrusted dagger, and Charles I's final choice of earring.

Twelfth Fragment

Josiah Wedgwood and William Blake

The Vase had really disappeared. It seems impossible to us, in an age of public galleries and colour supplements, that such a thing might happen, but at the end of the eighteenth century it could and did. Hamilton told his niece to convey the Vase to the Duchess 'secretly', and so successfully did she carry out this commission that even the Duchess's own family were not aware that she had acquired it. The Vase only saw the light of day after her death, two years later, when with the rest of her treasures it was exposed to the calculating gaze of the auctioneer.

When the Duchess died, her will revealed that she had left the contents of her museum to her younger son, with a suggestion that the collection could be sold, to compensate for the fact that the bulk of her vast estate would go to the eldest, the Third Duke of Portland. Her treasures were put up for auction the year after her death in more than four thousand lots, and chief among them was the Vase. A drawing was made, engraved as a frontispiece for the sale catalogue, intended to evoke a glimpse of the Duchess's museum. The picture shows a jumble of rare and valuable objects, heaped together in glorious disarray like the treasures of Tutankhamun's tomb. Among the china, books, coins and shells the Vase has pride of place, sitting centre-stage on a plinth. A mirror is propped behind it to show off the side of the frieze that would otherwise be hidden from view; hanging from the foot of the Vase is a drawing of the decoration on its base, and sticking out of its mouth is a large frond of coral, as though it were wearing an *outré* cocktail hat at a rather jaunty angle. The drawing is not to scale; the size of the Vase is greatly exaggerated, so that it appears to be the largest item in the collection, and it has been suggested that the objects were portrayed in the engraving not according to their actual size but rather to the prices they might realise. Copy for the catalogue was provided by the same Reverend John Lightfoot who had overseen the Duchess's botanical collections. His entry for the Vase gives us a good idea of the mixture of fact and misconception then surrounding it. He described it as

The most celebrated antique VASE, or SEPULCHRAL URN, from the Barberini Cabinet at Rome. It is the identical urn which contained the ashes of the Roman Emperor ALEXANDER SEVERUS, and his mother MAMMAEA which was deposited in the earth about the year 235 after Christ, and was dug up by order of POPE BARBERINI named URBAN VIII between the years 1623 and 1644.

With the excitement of the sale-room on him, Lightfoot let himself go a little:

> The materials of which it is composed emulate an onyx, the ground a rich transparent dark amethystine colour, and the snowy figures which adorn it are in bas-relief, of workmanship beyond all encomium, and such as cannot but excite in us the highest idea of the arts of the ancients.

And, it was to be hoped, invite the highest bids. Horace Walpole attended the sale, and gleefully anticipated a knock-down price: 'it will not, I conclude, produce half of what it cost the Duchess.' He was not quite correct. The sale lasted for six weeks, and the Vase came up on the penultimate day: 7 June 1786. It went under the hammer for 1026 pounds, making up nearly a tenth of the overall proceeds of the sale. It was sold to a 'Mr Tomlinson', but he was undoubtedly acting as an agent. At first the *Gentleman's Magazine* decided that the mystery buyer was the Duke of Marlborough, but a few weeks later it discovered and revealed the true identity of the Vase's new owner:

> The famous vase lately belonging to the Duchess of Portland is said to have been sold to a Mr Tomlinson for one thousand and twenty-six pounds. Readers may not be apprized that Mr T was a bidder for the Duke of Portland, and that his grace is the present owner of the curious relic of antiquity.

So the Duke, who had decided to keep the Vase in the family, had bid for it at the public auction, and in effect bought it from his brother. But the Duke had a rival bidder, someone with the resources to compete in the auction room and an obsession with vases that went far beyond the Duke's own. There is a story that the Duke only prevented his rival from bidding against him by agreeing to lend him the Vase for a year after the auction. This rival bidder was Josiah Wedgwood, the potter, and while the story of his threat to bid may be apocryphal, there is no doubting his desire to possess the Vase. Wedgwood and the Portland Vase were made for each other.

The sculptor John Flaxman saw the Vase when Hamilton first brought it to London, and at the beginning of February 1784 he wrote to Wedgwood about it:

> I wish you may soon come to town to see William Hamilton's vase. It is the finest production of Art that has been brought to England and seems to be the very apex of perfection to which you are endeavouring to bring your bisque & jasper; it is of a kind called 'Murrina' by Pliny, made of dark glass with white enamel figures. The vase is about a foot high and the figures between four and five inches, engraved in the same manner as a cameo and of the grandest and most perfect Greek sculpture.

Flaxman and Wedgwood had already collaborated on ceramics that look as if they had been directly inspired by the Vase itself, and this before they had ever laid eyes on it. Flaxman expected that Wedgwood would be excited by the Vase, but he can hardly have known what an obsession it would become, or that he himself would soon be spending so much time and effort diligently recreating these 'most perfect' figures.

Wedgwood had commissioned Flaxman to create the ornaments for his own vases and in 1778 Flaxman produced his most important bas-relief design for Wedgwood, 'The Apotheosis of Homer'. The resemblance to the Portland Vase is striking – white figures in bas-relief on a blue background. But this is not a coincidence; the link with Hamilton was already established. The design for 'The Apotheosis of Homer' came from another ancient vase that Hamilton had acquired, and which he had sold, along with the rest of his of his first collection of vases, to the British Museum in 1772. Wedgwood studied both the prints from d'Hancarville's publication and the vases themselves, and their influence on him was considerable.

Wedgwood was making his vases of 'jasper', to which Flaxman refers in his letter. Jasper was Wedgwood's great invention, an entirely new kind of ceramic body, the most important innovation in ceramics since the creation of porcelain by the Chinese nearly a thousand years earlier. Wedgwood is a sort of super-hero of ceramics. He developed the highest technical skills of the potter, and he had a frightening appetite for hard work, a canny commercial instinct, and the inspiration of a true innovator. His energy was demonic – he would throw himself into a project until his health was endangered to the point of breakdown, and then bounce back, eager for the next challenge. During the building of his new factory he 'overworked' an injured knee while walking over the site, and decided to have his right leg amputated (at this time, one must remember, anaesthesia was to say the least rudimentary and antisepsis not yet understood). Three weeks later the stump was almost healed, as Wedgwood reported to his business-partner Bentley: 'The wound is not quite 2 inches by one and a 1/4, I measured it with the compasses this morning when I dressed it. Yes, I dressed it, for I have turned the Surgeon adrift and Sally and I are sole managers now.'

'Everything gives way to experiment' was one of Wedgwood's favourite principles. He brought the same fascinated, detailed attention to his work in the potteries as he did to his own healing stump. At the beginning of the 1770s Bentley was asking Wedgwood for something new for their London showroom. Wedgwood was then producing dark, austere vases that imitated natural stone – agate or basalt. Bentley considered these rather masculine and asked for a 'finer body', something in the neo-classical style that would appeal to 'the Ladies'. So Wedgwood and Bentley decided to produce cameos that accorded with the fashion, as dictated by the Adam brothers, for pastel shades – blue, green, pink, yellow. This was what the truly up-to-date boudoir ought to be wearing.

Neo-classical – that is to say, design influenced by the works of Ancient Greece and Rome – is a modern term that Wedgwood would not have recognised. He called it the 'true' or 'correct' style. In part it was a reaction against heavily ornamented rococo. The neo-classical style had strong political overtones, because it appealed to the emerging middle classes, and became a symbol of their struggle against the ruling landed aristocracy who were trying desperately to keep them in their place. As the archetypal self-made man, and a radical thinker, Wedgwood was a natural champion of the style. At this time he also began to collaborate with James Tassie. Tassie supplied Wedgwood with moulds of cameos and intaglios taken from antique gems that portrayed the gods and heroes of the classical world, and Wedgwood replied with moulds from his own stock. They were both catering to the growing demand in Britain for all things classical, and to begin with their relationship was one of friendly rivalry. But Wedgwood began to voice to Bentley anxieties about the relative merits of their work, and Tassie, if he had known, would surely have been deeply flattered: 'Mr Tassie and Voyez, between them, have made terrible depradations on our Seal Trade. The former by making them more beautifull, and the later by selling them cheaper.'

Voyez, tellingly not given the honour of a prefix, was Wedgwood's other rival, and an altogether more malign bugbear. Jean Voyez was a sculptor and modeller who had been taken on by Wedgwood in 1769. Six months after his arrival at the works he was convicted of stealing '11 Models of Clay val 5£., 15 Moulds of Clay val 50s., and 15 moulds of Plaister val 50s. Goods of Josiah Wedgwood.' He was sentenced to transportation for seven years, but the sentence seems later to have been remitted to five months' imprisonment and a public whipping. This was unfortunate for Wedgwood, because Voyez was not engaged in petty theft: he was an industrial saboteur of the most dangerous type. Only a year later Wedgwood discovered to his dismay that Voyez was now in the employ of a rival potter, Palmer, and supplying exactly the know-how that Palmer needed in order to compete with the Wedgwood wares. Wedgwood even contemplated paying Voyez a pension in order to protect his business. As he pointed out in a letter to his partner, Bentley: 'The Selling of a single Vase less per week through such competition would be a greater loss to us than paying him his wages for nothing.' Then he discovered that Voyez was marking his seals with the 'W&B' mark of Wedgwood and Bentley's products. Wedgwood, understandably, was inclined to resort to the law, but his legal advisers assured him that an action would fail, because a rustic Staffordshire jury, untutored in the wicked ways of the commercial world, would not be brought to understand the seriousness of the offence. Fortunately after a few years Voyez, who was not perhaps the kind of man to settle down anywhere, left England, and Wedgwood must have breathed a sigh of relief.

Despite these anxieties and distractions, at the beginning of the 1770s Wedgwood felt able to reply to Bentley's request for something new:

I have for some time past been reviewing my experiments, & find such Roots, such Seeds as would open and branch out wonderfully if I could nail myself down to the cultivation of them for a year or two. And the Foxhunter does not enjoy more pleasure from the chace, than I do from the prosecution of my experiments when I am fairly entered into the field.

It took Wedgwood four years of secret experimentation to perfect his new medium, all the while running the successful manufactory he had called 'Etruria', and with his formidable wife Sarah raising a family which – not counting those that did not survive infancy – eventually numbered seven children. He wrote,

> If I had more time and more heads I could do something – but as it is I must be content to do as well as I can. A man who is in the midst of a course of experiments should not be at home to anything or anybody else but that cannot be my case … I am allmost crazy.

Wedgwood was using barium in his new mixture, but he did not fully understand the nature of this ingredient. When fired the pieces would blister and crack for no apparent reason. The overlaid bas-reliefs would crack off. The whole process was very costly. After five thousand experiments over three years he was still unable confidently to predict the outcome, and vases always collapsed after firing. But Wedgwood persevered relentlessly to perfect his invention. He developed a secret technique of casting vases in a coarser form of the jasper, which was then given a thin coating of the finer ware – a piece of chicanery that has only recently been discovered, and which made possible the project of 'the Vase'.

When the Portland Vase arrived in London, jasper was already on its way to becoming the most successful ornamental ware ever produced, and Wedgwood was ready, as ever, for a fresh challenge. When the Vase disappeared into the Duchess's private museum Wedgwood had an illustration to study while the idea of copying the Vase germinated. It must have 'opened and branched out wonderfully'. Soon after the auction, once Wedgwood had arranged to borrow it from the Duke, the Vase set out on its travels once more. Perhaps Wedgwood transported the Vase personally, clutching the straw-filled box to protect the precious contents as he bumped along the turnpike. Or perhaps it went by water, on a horse-drawn barge, along the canals and waterways of England, through the flat green fields of the Midlands to the new factory. Water transport was essential to Wedgwood's business – the appalling condition of the roads in eighteenth-century England made it almost impossible to transport fragile goods of any description except by water. Wedgwood had dug a canal to his factory to link it to the waterways, and without it he would not have been able to distribute his wares.

The very name of Wedgwood's factory made explicit his intention to use the factory to reproduce the vases of classical antiquity. Etruria was the area of Italy inhabited by the ancient Etruscans; Wedgwood shared the then-current misapprehension that ancient pottery excavated in Italy was Etruscan, rather than Roman or Greek. This confusion was in part caused by the historical accident of some of the finest surviving Greek vases having been found in Etruscan tombs. Despite its classical name, Wedgwood's Etruria factory was thoroughly modern, even ahead of its time. Water provided not only the crucial transport links but also power, from a water-wheel. As well as its good location and practicality of design the factory had housing for the workers, who enjoyed the unheard-of advantage of a sickness benefit scheme. It might have seemed to Wedgwood as though the whole edifice had always been awaiting the arrival of the Vase.

Once the Vase was at the factory, and in Wedgwood's hands – literally – it's clear that touching and holding it stirred up the conflicting passions that drove him. After a fortnight's careful study he wrote to Sir William Hamilton, the middle-class entrepreneur adopting the obsequious tone of shopkeeper to wealthy patron:

> You will be pleased, I am sure, to hear what a treasure is just now put into my hands, I mean the exquisite Vase with which you enriched these islands, and which, now that we may call it the Portland Vase, I hope will never depart from it. His Grace

has generously lent it me to copy, and permitted me to carry it down to this place, where I stand much in need of your advice and directions.

Wedgwood's previous study of the illustrations of the Vase had encouraged him to imagine that he could successfully copy the designs. Now he had it in his hands the true nature of the Vase was apparent. It was a nasty surprise.

Now that I can indulge myself with full and repeated examinations of the original work itself, my crest is much fallen, and I should scarcely muster sufficient resolution to proceed if I had not, too precipitately perhaps, pledged myself to many of my friends to attempt it in the best manner I am able.

He realised that, working in ceramic rather than glass, he would not be able to recreate the exquisite effects achieved by the original craftsman. His jasper could not be cut as thinly, or produce the effects of transparency, the shading and depth. But Wedgwood seems to have taken an almost masochistic pleasure in the problems to be faced. They were insurmountable but he would, of course, surmount them. His insight, honesty and enthusiasm are impressive:

I dare confess to you sir, that I have at times wrought myself up to a certain degree of enthusiasm, in contemplating the beauties of this admirable work; and in those paroxysms am ready to cry out, that this single piece is alone a sufficient foundation for a manufactory, and that of no small extent; and then I begin to count how many different ways the Vase itself may be copied, to suit the tastes, the wants, and the purses of different purchasers.

Wedgwood called together his best craftsmen and artists to begin the process of reproducing the ornamentation on the Vase. Chief among them was John Flaxman, who had originally called Wedgwood's attention to the object. Flaxman came from a poor family. He was the son of a plaster-cast maker near Covent Garden, and showed a precocious talent for modelling and drawing. He enrolled in the newly established Royal Academy Schools, and soon made a name for himself. His reputation reached Wedgwood in his manufactory in the English midlands, via a visitor called Freeman, as Wedgwood reported to his partner, Bentley:

He is a great admirer of young Flaxman and has advised his Father to send him to Rome which he has promised to do. Mr Freeman says he knows young Flaxman is a Coxcomb, but does not think him a bit the worse for it or the less likely to be a great Artist.

Flaxman does not seem to have been too much of a 'Coxcomb'. The contemporary artist Joseph Nollekens called him 'Little Flaxman', not just because of his stooped figure – he suffered from curvature of the spine – but because of 'his fixity of ideas, his imaginative poverty, his tendency to lapse into the sentimental or melodramatic'. But perhaps Nollekens envied him his exceptional talents, for Flaxman became one of the most influential artists of his day.

The head of the ornamental department at Etruria was Henry Webber, the son of a Swiss sculptor, who had just signed a seventeen-year contract with Wedgwood. He also involved his chief modeller William Hackford, known as 'the ingenious boy', who was especially gifted in fine modelling, and who stayed in the service of the Wedgwood firm for sixty-three years. Closely supervised by Wedgwood himself, and by his son Josiah II, these men began to create the shapes of the figures. By June 1787 they were completed, and moulds created in which the ornaments could be recreated and applied to the surfaces of the vases. Wedgwood was already planning to send Webber and Flaxman off to Rome 'for the purpose of making Models, Drawings and other improvements in the Arts of Modelling and Designing'. But the body of the Vase was proving much more of a problem. Jasper was still a capricious medium. He confided his troubles to Hamilton:

> I must depend on an agent, whose effects are neither at my command, nor to be perceived at the time they are produced, viz. the action of fire on my compositions; a little more or a little less fire, and even the length of time employed in producing the same degree, will make a very material difference in this delicate operation.

Despite all his previous experiments and hard-won experience, Wedgwood still could not predict what would happen to his trial pieces once they went into the kiln. He created a new colour for jasper that would match the dark blue of the Vase. He had recently invented a pyrometer, an instrument to measure the high temperatures used during the firing process. Before he did so successful firings depended on the skill of the kiln-master, who would estimate the temperature in a kiln simply from observing the colour of the fire. Wedgwood was elected a Fellow of the Royal Society for this achievement, and it helped him greatly in his attempts to copy the Vase. Nevertheless, he could not get his new medium to behave itself. Once in the kiln the vases that had been so carefully and laboriously constructed from the unfired jasper would blister and crack and collapse.

Copying the Vase was proving to be the most laborious and infuriating undertaking Wedgwood had ever embarked upon. The old syndrome asserted itself. He drove himself towards ill health, and had to consult his doctor, complaining of pains in his head and 'a general weakness'. The physician prescribed a holiday, which Wedgwood agreed to take 'as soon as the Portland Vase is complete'. The Vase itself had gone back to the Duke of Portland after a twelve-month loan, but its remote, cool perfection must have been ever present to Wedgwood's mind, mocking his frustrated endeavours. A letter to his son gives us a glimpse of the obsessive attention that Wedgwood gave to the task:

I wish you to look at the left leg of Pluto between the calf and the ancle the latter of which is not seen, & compare it with a cast taken out of the mould taken from the vase itself ... this part is said to be too broad. If so, it must be narrowed a little.

It had become an affair of honour. He had orders for copies of the Vase from his patrons, but he insisted that the subscribers should be able to refuse the copies if they were not satisfied. The care he took over the states of mind of his craftsmen gives us a hint of his own churning emotions: he urged his son not to tell the men that twenty orders had been placed for copies, so as not to put them under any pressure.

Three years after he had begun, Wedgwood's experience, skill, and sheer stubborn perseverance finally paid off. In September 1789 he produced a copy by which his own perfectionist standards were satisfied. 'The prospect,' he wrote, 'brightens before me.' In the spring of 1790 he was ready to give his copy its first public outing. Having a good understanding of the relationship between publicity and celebrity, he went straight to the top. In May his vase was shown to Queen Charlotte herself, who had first established Wedgwood's reputation by commissioning from him at the beginning of his career a service of what became known as 'Queen's ware'. The vase 'pleased her very highly'. It was then displayed in a private exhibition at the house of Sir Joseph Banks, the President of the Royal Society. The *Gazetteer and New Daily Advertiser* breathlessly recorded the event:

> On Saturday night last there was a numerous conversazione at Sir Joseph Banks's, Soho-square, when Mr Wedgwood produced the great vase, manufactured by himself, in imitation of that superb one about four years ago exhibited in the Museum of her Grace the Duchess Dowager of Portland. It is most exquisitely finished, and allowed by all present, in point of look to be at least equal to the original, which was valued at two thousand five hundred pounds. The whole of the above vase is a composition of the most beautiful transparency, and does infinite credit to the artist. Beside Sir Joseph and a numerous company who attended on the above occasion, there were present Sir Joshua Reynolds, the Hon. Horace Walpole and several members of the Royal and Antiquarian Societies.

Sir Joshua Reynolds, President of the Royal Academy, signed an official certificate to approve the vase as 'a correct and faithful imitation both in regard to general effort and the most minute detail of parts'. Hamilton did not see the vase until a year later, in 1791, but he then communicated his reaction in a letter to Wedgwood: 'The sublime character of the Original is wonderfully preserved in your Copy & little more is wanting than the sort of transparency which your materials could not imitate ... In short I am wonderfully pleased with it.'

Hamilton's double-edged praise highlights the flaw in the whole project that Wedgwood could never eradicate, however many experiments he made: jasper, his chosen medium, was opaque and could not reproduce the beauty of the original glass. Moreover, the enterprise could in no way be considered a commercial success. Selling the few copies he made – only about thirty were produced during his lifetime – could not possibly compensate for the time and money he had spent. Wedgwood's son was sent on a promotional tour of Europe, during which the Princess of Orange admired his vase but did not buy it. In fact it seems that Wedgwood only sold ten copies, and he began to make disappointed remarks about the fact that his custom was not going to cover his costs. But these first copies of the Portland Vase were his masterpiece, the last and finest chapter in a remarkable career. They are still regarded as among the greatest technical achievements in English ceramics. They became the hallmark – literally – of Wedgwood quality. No other manufactory had ever attempted, let alone achieved, such a difficult commission, and they brought the name of Wedgwood lasting fame. The Portland Vase gave Wedgwood something to measure himself against, something that called forth all his abilities and qualities. It was what he was always looking for – his greatest challenge.

The Wedgwood factory continued to produce copies of the Portland Vase throughout the following century, but none came near to the standards achieved by Wedgwood himself. The statue of Josiah that stands outside the modern Wedgwood factory and museum in Barlaston has the distinctive shape of the Vase, to symbolise this most lasting, most important association.

*

When Wedgwood produced his first perfect copy of the Vase, the first person to see it was his friend Erasmus Darwin, the doctor and – the term must be used loosely – poet. Darwin immediately celebrated his friend's achievement in verse:

> Etruria! Next beneath thy magic hands
> Glides the quick wheel, the plastic clay expands,
> Nerved with fine touch, thy fingers (as it turns)
> Mark the nice bounds of vases, ewers and urns;

And pleased on WEDGWOOD ray your partial smile
A new Etruria decks Britannia's isle.
Charmed by your touch, the kneaded clay refines,
The biscuit hardens, the enamel shines,
Each nicer mould a softer feature drinks,
The bold cameo speaks, the soft intaglio thinks.

Whether, O Friend of Art! your gems derive
Fine forms from Greece, and fabled Gods revive;
Or bid from modern life the portrait breathe,
And bind round Honour's brow the laurel wreath;
Buoyant shall sail, with Fame's historic page,
Each fair medallion o'er the rocks of age.

These lines are from Darwin's long and ambitious poem *The Botanic Garden*, a mammoth work of over two thousand rhyming couplets. It was intended 'to induce the ingenious to cultivate the knowledge of Botany, by introducing them to the vestibule of that delightful science'. The poem was divided into two sections: in the first, 'the physiology of plants is delivered; and the operation of the elements, as far as they may be supposed to affect the growth of vegetables'. The second section dealt with the 'loves of the plants' and particularly 'the Sexual system of Linnaeus'. Although now merely a literary curiosity, at the time it was a great success, and in Darwin's defence it must be said that while he was producing these absurd and bombastic verses his tongue was often in his cheek. The lines above come from a section of the poem concerning the natural products of the earth in general, and pottery in particular. Having introduced his friend Wedgwood, Darwin went one stage further, and embarked on a lengthy digression concerning the Vase itself. When Wedgwood sent Darwin his first successful copy of the Vase, he had hinted that it 'might furnish even a minor poet with subjects for a few lines; what effect must it have then on a fancy and genius of the first order?' Darwin took the bait, and steered his poem into speculation 'O'er the fine forms on PORTLAND's mystic urn'.

Darwin's metaphysical interpretation of the figures on the Vase was further explained in an eleven-page footnote, the gist of which was that the Vase showed the journey from life to death of all mankind. Fortunately in the poem itself this was more economically expressed:

> *Here* fall'n columns and disjoin'd arcades,
> On mouldering stones, beneath deciduous shades,
> Sits HUMANKIND in hieroglyphic state,
> Serious, and pondering on their changeful state.

(This refers to figures E and G, as it were male and female representatives of the human race.)

> While with inverted torch, and swimming eyes,
> Sinks the fair shade of MORTAL LIFE, and dies.

(This is figure F.)

> *There* the pale GHOST though death's wide portal bends
> His timid feet, the dusky steep descends;

(Figure A.)

> With smiles assuasive LOVE DIVINE invites,
> Guides on broad wing, with torch uplifted lights:

(This is Cupid.)

> IMMORTAL LIFE, her hand extending, courts
> The lingering form, his tottering step supports;

(Figure C.)

> Leads on to Pluto's realm the dreary way,
> And gives him trembling to Elysian day.

(Figure D, therefore, is Pluto.)

The identification of Figure C as 'Immortal Life' is supported in the footnote – 'by her fondling between her knees a large and playful serpent, which from its annually renewing its external skin has from great antiquity ... been esteemed an emblem of renovated youth'. Darwin also supplies an interpretation for the figure on the base disc:

> *Beneath,* in sacred robes the priestess dress'd,
> The coif close-hooded, and the fluttering vest,
> With pointing finger guides the initiate youth,
> Unweaves the many-coloured veil of Truth,
> Drives the profane from Mystery's bolted door,
> And Silence guards the Eleusinian lore.

Darwin's theory is at least refreshingly different, and it is certainly the only one to be formulated in rhyming couplets. Wedgwood himself took it up, and added a few refinements of his own; he pointed out that the column standing behind Figure E 'with its capital thrown down at the feet of this emblem of death may denote that the person deceased was the head of a great family, as so costly an urn would only be purchased by persons of the first rank'. He speculated that the staff held by Figure G might 'be an emblem of the authority of the deceased'. He was particularly taken with the interpretation of Figure A as the soul entering the next world: 'The timidity with which the new guest takes his first steps out of this portal, his holding fast to his garment, beautifully denotes the reluctance with which he puts off his corporeal existence.'

Darwin wanted pictures of the Vase for his epic footnote – four of the eleven pages were to be plates illustrating his theory. He knew that the Vase had been drawn by Cipriani and engraved by Bartolozzi, and asked his publisher if he could use the resulting plates. Darwin's publisher, Johnson, was worried about copyright; they could not be copied without Hamilton's consent. But Johnson had another suggestion, concerning one of the engravers who worked for him on a freelance basis: 'Blake is certainly capable of making an exact copy of the Vase, I believe more so than Mr Bartolozzi, if the Vase were lent to him for that purpose, & I see no other way of its being done.' So, by mere coincidence, in the autumn of 1791 the Vase had its most unexpected and remarkable encounter, with one of the great visionary artists of any age: William Blake.

The Vase was now famous, an A-list celebrity of classical art. Blake was a nobody who lived out his life in obscurity and often penury, his poetic and artistic genius unrecognised. The Vase had never encountered Blake before, nor anyone like him, but Blake was no stranger to the Vase. He had long been influenced by the artworks of the classical past. As a child, he attended a drawing school in the Strand, run by Henry Pars. Pars's brother William had been commissioned by the Society of Dilettanti to sketch ancient statues and buildings in Greece and Asia Minor – his *Ionian Antiquities* was published when Blake was in his second year at the school, and the fragments and ruins it portrayed sank into Blake's mind. He studied casts of famous classical statues, and acquired copies. Some of these subsequently turned up in his work – Hercules as 'Giant Despair' in his illustrations of Bunyan, for example. He began to buy prints and engravings, and discovered a predilection for Raphael.

In 1772, at the age of fourteen, he was apprenticed to an engraver, James Basire. Basire was working on commissions from the Society of Antiquaries, and had collaborated with Pars. Under him, Blake learnt the arduous trade of the engraver, and helped with his master's commissions, including illustrations for the publication *Archaeologia: Or Miscellaneous Tracts Relating to Antiquity*. Shortly before the Vase came into Blake's hands, two learned antiquarians aired their opposing theories concerning the figures on the Vase in this very compendium. J. G. King linked his theory to Alexander Severus; for him the figures A-D were 'an allusion to the birth of Alexander the

Great under which is typified the birth of Alexander Severus'. Figure A was Alexander the Great and/or Alexander Severus. Figure C was either or both of the mothers of these two, Olympias and/or Mammaea, and Figure D was Jupiter. On the other side of the Vase, King fancied he detected a reference to Alexander Severus's building projects; figure E is the Emperor again, and the rocks on which he sits are a 'bath', to symbolise the Roman baths built during his reign. Figure F is Mammaea again, though King resists the temptation to suggest that her up-ended torch is in fact a loofah, and figure G is 'Constancy'.

This is arbitrary enough, but it sounds like pure reason compared to the theory then put forward in the same publication by a fellow antiquarian named Marsh. For the first side of the Vase, Marsh followed his colleague, but the second side was, he decided, a play on 'scattered features of well-known history, satyrically sketched out'. This 'satire' compared Alexander Severus with his predecessor, Elagabalus, 'to lash a luxurious emperor, addicted to the most shameful vices, and to praise a virtuous one'. Elagabalus – figure E – 'sits with his garment loose, in attitude slothful, obscene and libidinous'. It never seems to cross Marsh's mind that all the male figures on the Vase, and indeed all classical statues, behave with rather less 'modesty' than trouser-wearing modern man. 'At his feet female or connubial love [figure F] lies sorrowful.' Marsh is referring to Elagabalus's homosexuality, but can't quite bring himself to state the matter openly: Figure F might also represent 'a most beautiful woman, rejected and repudiated by that monster of impurity; and we know the causes of that repudiation'. Figure G is 'a female monitor, divination, revolving many things in her mind, fixed in purpose, leaning firmly, perhaps, on an augural lituus, just going to give a response to the tyrant, or, like another Syrian priestess, ready to denounce his death'.

Blake also acquired a copy of Winckelmann's *Reflections on the*

Painting and the Sculpture of the Greeks, and was influenced by his ideals. In 1779 he joined the Royal Academy, which founded its teaching on classical art. Key textbooks at the Academy included William Hamilton's publication of his vases, as designed by d'Hancarville, and Montfaucon's *L'Antiquité expliquée*, which included his interpretation of the figures on the Vase as referring to the myth of Leda and the swan. In the same year Blake met fellow artist John Flaxman. Both were Londoners, both the sons of tradesmen. Flaxman was already working for Wedgwood and would go on to help with his copy of the Vase and become the most celebrated artist of his day – the very opposite of Blake's fate. But despite this, and despite Blake's prickly, highly eccentric nature, they remained on friendly terms for many years.

The works that Blake studied stimulated a love of the ancient world, and his imagination responded powerfully, delighting to project itself back over the vast stretches of time to a remote antiquity. Blake's biographer Peter Ackroyd suggests that his love of the deep past was linked to a preoccupation with death, and suggests that Blake wanted somehow to lose himself in the ancient world. In 1789, Blake's youngest brother died, probably of tuberculosis. He was Blake's beloved favourite, and Blake had been training him as a draughtsman. Blake sat beside the deathbed for a fortnight as Robert struggled through the ghastly final stages of the disease, and at the end saw Robert's spirit rising through the ceiling, 'clapping its hands for joy'. After Robert's death Blake began to read the works of Emmanuel Swedenborg, whose philosophy included a firm belief in a resurrection of the dead in spiritual but also perfect human form.

Blake had taken up engraving to earn a living while still studying at the Academy. It became his trade, and he was never able to give it up. It was drudgery, but he stuck to it, to support himself and his wife Catherine. But after Robert's death he used the technical knowledge of his trade to create an entirely new medium. Just before he met the

Vase, he produced *Songs of Innocence*, in which the poems and illustrations were all etched directly onto the engraver's plate to form an unprecedented whole. This technique was, according to Blake's early biographer J. T. Smith, inspired by Robert:

> His brother Robert stood before him in one of his visionary imaginations, and so decidedly directed him in the way in which he ought to proceed, that he immediately followed his advice, by writing his poetry, and drawing his marginal subjects of embellishments in outline upon the copper plate.

It was the beginning of a burst of creativity, and soon after, he produced *Songs of Experience*, with its 'Tyger, Tyger', the poems drafted out in the back of Robert's notebook, which was carefully preserved and re-used.

Between these two first-fruits and masterworks of his extraordinary vision, Blake undertook his commission from Johnson, and engraved the Vase. What did he think as he examined the first figure on the frieze, the perfect figure of the young man who was, according to Darwin's interpretation, a ghost entering the afterlife? He may have disapproved of the 'reluctance' with which the ghost 'puts off his corporeal existence'. But otherwise Darwin's interpretation must have appealed to him, bound up as he was with his brother's spirit-journey to the next world. As he sharpened his needle or burin, rested his copper plate on its leather cushion, gazed at the frieze and began his work, he was at least able to compare the scenes on the Vase with his own extraordinary visions.

Thirteenth Fragment
The Dukes of Portland and the Duchess of Gordon

The Vase had been bought by 'Mr Tomlinson' at auction at the premises of Skinner and Company in Aldersgate Street in July 1785, had been sent on loan to Wedgwood for a year, and finally came fully into the possession of the Third Duke of Portland in 1786. From now on it began to be known as the Portland Vase. The origins of the dukedom which gave its name to the Vase lie in the affections of King William III. When William was Prince of Orange, an obscure if determined player in the seventeenth-century European conflict between Protestants and Catholics, his page was one William Bentinck, a fellow Netherlander. In 1675 the young Prince William contracted smallpox, and during this potentially fatal and highly contagious illness, Bentinck nursed his friend and master. This early proof of devotion cemented what would be a thirty-year friendship, and rather more than that; it was the beginning of a serious relationship. The Prince of Orange and William Bentinck were lovers.

When the increasing unpopularity of the Catholic James II prompted ambassadors from England to offer the crown to the Prince of Orange, Bentinck was the trusted confidant given the task of negotiating. He helped to arrange the strategic marriage between Prince William and Mary Stuart, daughter of James II, and he oversaw the detailed planning of the invasion of England by troops loyal to William and the Protestant cause. This virtually bloodless and entirely successful coup put William on the English throne, and one of his first acts as king was to make his friend Groom of the Stool, First Gentleman of the Bedchamber (never was the title more fittingly given or held) and Earl of Portland. The measure of the favouritism William displayed towards Bentinck can be detected in the jealous animosity it stimulated. His closeness to the King made Bentinck distrusted and disliked by those denied the royal ear:

> The King thinks
> The Queen tells
> The Princess eats
> Prince George drinks
> Lord Portland takes – all things.

This was a piece of envious doggerel current at the time, and apart from commemorating the various foibles of the royal family, it demonstrates how great King William's generosity to his friend was. The more jealous and suspicious the English aristocracy showed themselves to be, the more the King favoured his friend who, he knew, had his interests at heart. They fought together at the battle of the Boyne, and at Landen. (William was not a very successful military commander, but there is no doubting his courage and persistence. On one occasion, when wounded on the battlefield in the sight of his troops, instead of quietly retiring to seek medical attention he stayed on the field, taking off his hat and waving it vigorously to prevent the spread of alarm and despondency in the ranks.) Bentinck was instrumental in frustrating an assassination attempt on William, and was rewarded with yet more grants of land.

Bentinck was honest, direct, devoted, but he was a long-term boyfriend, not a courtier, and he could not cope with the arrival at court of young Arnold Joost van Keppel, who became the King's new favourite. Van Keppel was all youthful charm and high spirits; the King doted on him, and Bentinck was stricken with jealousy. He retired from court in a sulk which lasted for years, and was only reconciled with William when the King lay on his deathbed. Summoned to his side, Bentinck arrived when his master was beyond speech, but the King took Bentinck's hand and pressed it to his heart, in a touching gesture of forgiveness and love.

The Bentinck family took root in the many acres of English soil granted them by King William, and flourished. Bentinck's son was made a duke by George I. He was also offered the governorship of Jamaica, a less comfortable gift, and one he was only induced to take after having lost significant amounts of money in the South Sea Bubble. Englishmen had a habit of dying young in the West Indies, and the First Duke of Portland was no exception; he lasted four years in the job before being carried off by the Yellow Jack, or some other scourge of the colonial constitution, at the age of forty-four. His son, the Second Duke, thus inherited the title while still a teenager. He was very handsome, and was eventually elected a Fellow of the Royal Society, but most importantly, in 1734 he married Margaret Cavendish Holles-Harley, avid collector of curiosities and subsequent purchaser of the Vase, and he retired into a quiet, domestic, rural existence with her. It was his son, William Cavendish-Bentinck, the Third Duke of Portland, who bought the Vase at auction after his mother's death, and became its owner for the next twenty-five years.

William Cavendish-Bentinck had a traditional career as a young aristocrat. He went up to Oxford, and took his M.A. He did the Grand Tour and spent nearly three years in Italy, although there is no evidence that he ever visited the Palazzo Barberini to view his future acquisition. He learned to drink like his peers – that is, to excess – and by the age of twenty-six was consuming two bottles of claret daily, and perhaps not surprisingly suffering the first twinges of gout. On the death of his father in 1761 he inherited the dukedom, and took his place in the House of Lords. He had love affairs, first with Maria Walpole, Countess of Waldegrave, a niece of Horace Walpole. Maria was a beautiful widow, but she had her sights set on a higher prospect even than William; she soon threw him over for the Duke of Gloucester, brother to George III, to whom she was subsequently married in secret. William had another romantic entanglement with a married woman, the plaintive Anne Liddell, Duchess of Grafton, who was ill treated by her husband (he neglected her for his own notorious mistress) and poured out her woes to her confidant. News of William's engagement gave her a 'Confusion of Sentiments', but she tried her best to be pleased for her 'friend'.

William married another Cavendish, Dorothy, daughter of the Fourth Duke of Devonshire. It was a good marriage from the dynastic point of view, but it also proved successful on purely personal terms, being long and happy. William began to take on the business of overseeing his extensive properties. He took his responsibilities seriously, and was soon plunged in correspondence dealing with rents, leases, tithes, roads, livestock, crops, buildings and even mines, of which he owned several. The expenses of his estates always seemed to swallow up the income. William had a younger brother, Edward, a classic black sheep and ne'er-do-well, whose nickname 'Jolly Heart' perhaps explains his elder brother's constant indulgence. William remonstrated with him: 'I have always been bred to think that society has its claims,' he wrote to his brother, but as far as Edward was concerned the race-course had its claims too, and that was that. Edward sank into bankruptcy and fits, and William continued to pay his bills. Horace Walpole condemned him for having 'too great compassion for an idle and worthless younger brother', but Horace was a late addition to the Walpole family, and never loved his own siblings. William's generosity was almost as damaging as his incompetence; he nobly excused a friend from honouring a debt of thirty-six thousand pounds, a truly colossal sum. William, despite his best efforts and the vast resources at his disposal, was not good with money. He had run up debts at Oxford, prompting some anxious letters from his mother the Duchess, and continued to do so. Now they began to quarrel; he had power of attorney, but she insisted on issuing orders. And all the while, she was spending her own substantial income on her curiosities and menageries, not to mention nearly two thousand pounds on one Vase.

They also fell out over politics. Having 'been bred to think that society has its claims', William took his seat in the House of Lords, and an active part in its doings and the eternal warfare between the Whig and Tory parties. William joined the Whigs, as was only natural; they were an oligarchy of the landed interest. But their power was eclipsed by the arrival of George III on the throne; he was determined to put down party politics, and claw back power to the monarchy. His greatest ally in Parliament was the Count of Bute (by all accounts a pompous idiot, but entirely trusted by the King), whose wife happened to be best friends with the Duchess of Portland. The

Duchess followed her friend rather than her son, and was not amused by his Whiggish tendencies. She wrote accordingly: 'I must desire you will inform me if you intend to support the King's measures or join the Opposition. If your Connections or Engagements induce you to that resolution I can only say I am sorry for it.' But he did, and she was. Indeed, by 1782, he was leader of the Whigs, having served his party to the best of his ability, and earned the respect of its leading lights.

But these leading lights were, specifically, Edmund Burke and Charles James Fox, and their differing reactions to the French Revolution split the Whig party. Fox greeted the Revolution with enthusiasm. Burke, in his famous 'Reflections on the French Revolution', condemned it. William, who was deeply under the spell of Fox's brilliance and charm, but felt instinctively that Burke was right, was pulled apart along with the party. In 1792, with the Revolution now descending into a chaos of massacre and war, representatives of the party waited on William, coming to demand that he separate himself and the party from the friend and political ally he admired beyond all others – Fox. One of those present described William's pained and painful reaction:

> To all this, strange as it may appear, the Duke of Portland replied nothing, neither would he answer a word ... I, although I have often seen him benumbed and paralysed, never saw him or anyone else, so completely so before. All was one dead silence on his part; he seemed in a trance, and nothing could be so painful as these two hours, for our conversation lasted as long as that, reckoning intervals of ten and fifteen minutes' silence.

In these days of professional politicians, never at a loss for a well-turned sound bite, there is something striking about this picture of a man, thrust mainly by an accident of birth into a position for which he does not seem to have been fully qualified, struck dumb by contending thoughts and emotions and his own embattled integrity. In the end, William bowed to the inevitable, broke with Fox, and led his followers over to help the Tory government in the bloody struggle with Revolutionary and then Napoleonic France. He gained the office of Secretary of State, and eventually became First Lord of the Treasury. In 1807, in his seventies and now a sympathetic friend of the ailing King, William was Prime Minister, although for the entire length of his premiership he never so much as opened his mouth in Parliament. He died in 1809. He left a reputation as being, in Horace Walpole's words, 'a proud though bashful man'. He also left debts of half a million pounds, and, of course, the Vase.

It is not clear exactly where the Vase lived during its ownership by the Third Duke. It stayed in his keeping for twenty-three years, and although it was not kept so secret as it had been in the Duchess's museum, nevertheless it led a very private life. It may have been at Bulstrode or Welbeck, or on show at the Duke's London house, where it would be most admired by his political cronies and the society of the capital. What is known for certain is that at some point during William's ownership of the Vase, it was cracked. There is no record of exactly when or how this happened, but the culprit was named; some time at the end of the eighteenth century the Vase suffered damage at the hands of Jane, Duchess of Gordon. Jane was a political enemy of William, a staunch and active Tory, and any meeting between the two would therefore have been coloured by their political rivalry. She may not actually have used the Vase as a weapon in the political debate, but knowledge of Jane's character and background does go some way towards explaining why she might be responsible for the carelessness, clumsiness or wildness that resulted in its damage.

*

Until now the actors in the story of the Vase have fallen into two main categories: those who owned it, and those who studied it. But there is a third category: those who damaged the Vase. Chief among these is William Mulcahy, but he is not alone: between the time the Third Duke of Portland came to possess the Vase and the present day, no fewer than four people, for very different reasons, have been responsible for violating to a greater or lesser extent its pristine fragility, and the Duchess of Gordon was merely the first of these. Exactly what she did – whether she dropped it, or pushed it over, or knocked against it– is obscure. The damage was relatively minor, and cannot now be distinguished from later cracks. All that is known for certain is that the Vase suffered a 'fracture' at her hands. This fracture affected the base of the Vase, which came right off and had to be fixed back onto the body. Perhaps it was nothing worse than an unlucky accident, but the truth is that the Duchess had a reputation for wild and extravagant behaviour of all sorts, which was founded during her childhood in genteel poverty, fostered by a romantic story of star-crossed love, and cemented by an adult career of vaulting ambition and extraordinary political influence.

The Duchess of Gordon was born plain Jane Maxwell, daughter to a baronet with little money or position. She was brought up in a small flat in Edinburgh, where underclothes hung drying in the dark passages, or were slung out of the window on a pole. She and her sister Eglantine fetched water for the tea-kettle from the communal pump in the courtyard. One of their favourite childhood occupations was to ride on the backs of pigs, which were still allowed to browse the streets of eighteenth-century Edinburgh. A contemporary records how 'an old gentleman who was their relation told me that the first time he saw these beautiful girls was in the High Street, where Miss Jane was riding upon a sow which Miss Eglintoune thumped lustily behind with a stick'. What characterised the Maxwell girls, apart from their poverty and high spirits, was their good looks.

Jane was especially blessed, with dark expressive eyes, regular features and a peculiar grace. While still a teenager she provided the inspiration for a song, 'Jenny of Monreith', and was celebrated as 'the Flower of Galloway'. Unfortunately, the tragic events of her early adult life also sound as though they have been drawn from the most hackneyed ballad. She fell in love with a young officer who was posted overseas. When word came that he had been killed, Jane was devastated. In grief and despair, she went through with a loveless but otherwise ideal marriage to the Duke of Gordon, who was not only wealthy but also one of the handsomest men of his day. Then, during the honeymoon, Jane received a letter from – oh horror! – her lost love, to say that he was alive and well, and on the way home to claim her. Distracted, she fled from her husband, collapsed, and was found, along with her lover's letter, which the Duke then read.

The marriage does not seem to have properly recovered from this romantic but rocky start. Jane dutifully produced seven children, but the Duke fathered another nine outside the marriage. Aside from this impressive fertility, he was 'a man of easy habits and mediocre abilities' who preferred to spend his time on his country estates, engaged in rural affairs, field sports and the breeding of deer hounds. At least once, however, he succumbed to the epidemic of song-writing of which Jane seems to have been an epicentre, by composing what became a well-known ditty called 'There's Cauld Kail in Aberdeen'. ('Kail' or cabbage was, according to the *Oxford English Dictionary*, 'long the chief element of dinner in Scotland' and therefore 'used to denote the meal itself'. Why it should be of such a low temperature in Aberdeen is not clear.)

But Jane's natural, hog-thumping, Vase-cracking high spirits were not extinguished by her marriage to the Duke; rather, they seem to have been exaggerated to an almost demonic level, as she sought to forget her cares in gaiety and excitement. Her manners and conversation were unbridled: according to a contemporary, 'Her conversation bore a very strong analogy to her intellectual formation. Exempted by her sex, rank and beauty from those restraints imposed on women by the generally recognised usages of society the Duchess of Gordon frequently dispensed with their observance.' She became a socialite, a hostess, an 'Empress of fashion', as Horace Walpole described her in 1791, marvelling at her frenetic pace:

> I heard her journal of last Monday. She first went to Handel's music in the Abbey, then she clambered over the benches and went to Hastings' trial in the Hall; after dinner, to the play, then to Lady Lucan's Assembly; after that to Ranelagh, and returned to Mrs Hobart's faro-table; gave a ball herself in the evening of that morning into which she must have got a good way; and set out for Scotland the next day. Hercules could not have achieved a quarter of her labours in the same space of time.

Having had her own romantic ambitions destroyed, when her daughters grew up Jane directed all her energy to arranging advantageous marriages for them. She became notorious for this, and 'eligible bachelors' would go into hiding when she made her visit, trembling in the knowledge that she would stop at nothing to ensnare them. When she was attempting to secure a marriage for her fourth daughter, who had sadly not inherited her beauty, the father of the bridegroom, Lord Cornwallis, objected to the union on the grounds that the Gordon blood was tainted by madness. This was not unfounded: Lord George Gordon's increasingly unorthodox behaviour had sparked the anti-Catholic Gordon Riots, and now manifested itself in conversion to Judaism, a floor-length grey beard, and the name Israel Abraham George Gordon. Jane removed this problem at a stroke by confidentially informing Lord Cornwallis that 'Louisa has not a drop of Gordon blood in her veins'. This is perhaps fair enough, when the Duke's extra-marital record is taken into account; in any case it seems to have satisfied Lord Cornwallis, for the marriage went ahead. Her eldest daughter, Charlotte, married the Duke of Richmond. Susan became the Duchess of Manchester. Georgina was engaged to Francis, the Fifth Duke of Bedford, but when he died from 'an over-exertion at tennis', Jane secured a transfer to his brother, the Sixth Duke, and Georgina duly became the Duchess of Bedford a year later.

Not content with this staggering domestic success, Jane went into politics, taking the Tory side in the war with the Whigs, and in the battle between the Tory Prime Minister William Pitt and his great Whig rival, Fox. Jane worked as unofficial whip for her chosen party, using her charms to rally supporters to Pitt's government, and if charm failed she was not above bullying and intimidation. Her most remarkable achievement in the political field was her relationship with the Prime Minister Pitt himself, which – without being scandalous – grew very close. She became his familiar and eventually even his confidante. It gave her real political influence, and it is perhaps the most telling tribute to her extraordinary nature, at a time when members of her sex rarely had access to power of this sort.

It has been suggested that the Vase went to the British Museum partly because of Jane's carelessness, that it was deposited there after the death of the Third Duke in order to protect it from the kind of casual damage that was inflicted on it while in the Duke's private house. When the Third Duke died in 1809, the Vase became the property of his son, William Henry, now the Fourth Duke of Portland. Only a year after he inherited it, William Henry gave the Vase into the keeping of the British Museum. It arrived there just after the Rosetta Stone and just before the Elgin Marbles. The Museum was in a great period of expansion, with treasures flowing in from all over the world as British adventurers, ambassadors, explorers and archaeologists quartered the globe, armed with the confidence and wealth of a growing empire. But it was only a loan; William Henry kept ownership of the Vase, and must have viewed it as an important part of his inheritance. If he had not he would certainly have sold it. He had no compunction, for instance, about selling Bulstrode, so beloved of his grandmother the Duchess and her companion Mrs Delany. He was making heroic efforts to pay off the gigantic debts that his improvident father had allowed to accumulate, and it is greatly to his credit that he did not automatically seize on the Vase as a way of providing at least a small part of the half-million pounds he needed in order to put himself back into the black.

Fortunately, William Henry was significantly more successful with money than his father, and he had luck as well as judgement; as London swelled to monstrous proportions with power, population and money, he watched the rental value of his extensive holdings in Marylebone go through the roof. He was not a miser, or a slave-driver; he looked after his tenants and his flocks, and they all increased and multiplied. He tended his forests, improved the drainage in his meadows, introduced progressive farming techniques, and invested in his coal mines and his railways. Within a remarkably short space of time the debts were paid, and none of this prevented William Henry from vigorously pursuing other interests as well. He became obsessed with shipbuilding, and championed the cause of a ship-designer, Symonds. By funding the construction of a vessel on Symonds's principles, and offering to race it against the navy's best, he persuaded the Admiralty to take notice of Symonds's ideas. His ship, the *Pantaloon,* beat the crack naval frigate *Barham* hands down, and in the teeth of a reactionary Admiralty, Symonds went on to build the last generation of the Royal Navy's sailing vessels before the advent of steam.

Like his uncle Edward, William Henry was fond of the turf. He frequented Newmarket in a wagon specially fitted with a telescope through which he could follow the progress of the race, although – perhaps with Uncle 'Jolly Heart's' awful example before him – he never laid a wager. He owned a Derby winner, Tiresias, and built the Portland Stand at Newmarket. He lived on into his eighties, still vigorous, alert, kindly, and careful with money, insisting that no more than a hundred pounds should be spent on his funeral. He died the day that Britain declared war on Russia and the Crimean debacle began, in 1854. William Henry could be displayed as a figure of continuity, order and progress, of tradition and good management: settled, solid and safe. So it is perhaps ironic that it was during the period of his ownership that the Vase suffered worst. It was William Henry who received the letter from the British Museum trustees, notifying him of the 'lamentable occurrence' in 1845 when the Vase was smashed, and who wrote back with such forbearance, dissuading them from pursuing Mulcahy's family for 'an act of folly or madness which they could not control'.

Fourteenth Fragment

Doubleday, Windus and the Fifth Duke of Portland

In February 1845 the Vase lay in fragments, but after these had been carefully gathered up and examined, the possibility of restoration looked slightly less than hopeless. Some of the figures had only been broken into large pieces, pieces with unsplintered edges. The base disc was almost unharmed, although the handles were in a bad state. All in all, the Museum considered a restoration attempt worthwhile, and the Duke gave his consent.

The Museum entrusted the work to one of their in-house craftsmen, John Doubleday. His first act was to commission a watercolour of the fragments, which would stand as a record of the enormity of his task. The two hundred and more pieces were arranged in a rectangular frame. In the centre lay the base disc, unharmed. Below it were laid the larger, less damaged pieces from the side of the Vase showing the figure of the reclining woman – indeed, that figure is clearly distinguishable – and above were laid the more fragmented pieces from the other side of the Vase, of which only a hand or face is recognisable here and there. Between these two, flanking the disc, a host of tiny fragments were carefully positioned, many of them from the bases of the handles, and on either side of these were placed two small circular containers in which were hundreds of tiny splinters. A more intimidating jigsaw puzzle could scarcely be imagined, but by September of the following year Doubleday had completed his task to such good effect that the Vase was once more put on show in the Museum. The *Gentleman's Magazine* lauded 'the cleverness with which he has in a great degree contrived to render imperceptible the innumerable lines of conjunction' and hailed Doubleday as 'the prince of restorers'. The Museum awarded him a bonus of twenty-five pounds. There is a photograph of him, a marvellous 'before and after' composition, in which he sits in front of the watercolour of the fragments, while the restored Vase perches beside him on the corner of a table. He stares with narrowed eyes and beetling brows at the watercolour, as though still calculating how he will solve the giant puzzle, but has his arm around the restored Vase in a gesture of conquest.

*

Even before its restoration the Duke of Portland accepted the destruction of the Vase with fortitude and a spirit of forgiveness. The

[170]

readers of the *Times* were less forbearing: one wrote in to suggest the return of the stocks, and another, identifying himself only as 'F. S. A.', prescribed 'public whipping' for Mulcahy and his like. This latter correspondent was almost certainly Thomas Windus, Fellow of the Society of Antiquaries, who had just published a monograph, *A New Elucidation of the Subjects on the Celebrated Portland Vase*. After the destruction of the Vase he printed an addendum to this work, giving further voice to his outrage. He, like the Duke, was concerned to keep Mulcahy's identity secret: 'In common charity and good feeling let us drop tears on the catastrophe, and blot out the name of the perpetrator for ever.' But despite these fine words his motive for concealing that name was less charitable than the Duke's. He wrote,

Suffer it not for the sake of notoriety to be handed down to posterity as that of Eratostratus, the Ephesian, who burnt the famous temple of Diana, at Ephesus, on the day of the birth of Alexander the Great. The infliction of a severe public flagellation for injuries committed on the fine arts would tend much to cauterise these phrenological mischievous sensations from breaking out into active violence.

Windus was the sort of man for whom the phrase 'pompous ass' could have been invented. He had already written to the *Gentleman's Magazine* to tell the world 'what I conceive the best mode of restoring it partially to its original character and shape'. He suggested acquiring a copy of the Vase and scraping off the figures: 'It will then be in a proper state and size to receive the original fragments remaining, which can be easily secured with cement.' He had also finally, so he fondly believed, hit on the correct interpretation of the figures on the Vase: 'The whole allegory blazed on me at once in union with my favourite hypothesis – the sexes correct – and all the attributes ...

from the excitement I exclaimed with all the ardour of Archimedes, EUREKA! EUREKA!'

Windus decided that Figure D on the Vase had 'a medical appearance'. Unfortunately he does not specify what ancient equivalent to the stethoscope or white coat convinced him of this, but having laid his foundations in the sand, he researched the biographies of ancient physicians and went on to build a tall but shaky structure. He decided that Figure D was Galen, a famous doctor of second-century Rome, and the scenes on the Vase celebrated Galen's cure of the daughter of the Emperor Marcus Aurelius. According to the story, the Princess was suffering from a mysterious and incurable malady, until Galen, summoned by the desperate emperor, determined that she was merely lovesick. She had conceived a passion for a rope-dancer called Pylades, and as soon as he was introduced into the sickroom she made a miraculous recovery. Figure F on the Vase is the Princess, pining for her dancer, while the imperial parents sit anxiously on either side. Figure C is the Princess recovered, fondling 'the gyrating Hygeian Serpent, emblem of healing'. Galen, figure D, looks on with professional satisfaction, while figure A, the rope-dancer, advances towards his admirer. Once you imagine that figure A is indeed a kind of circus performer it is absurdly possible to detect in his posture something of the acrobat, moving with balanced steps towards his love as though on a tightrope.

At least, as Windus points out, his theory successfully accommodates the sexes of the figures, and this alone puts him above some of his predecessors. But there is one fatal flaw in his theory: as we will see, the Vase was in fact created two hundred years before Galen made his reputation and the Princess fell in love.

In 1854, after the death of the Fourth Duke of Portland, the Vase was inherited by his son John, who duly became the Fifth Duke. John kept up the loan of the Vase to the British Museum, where it stayed, restored and on display again. The damage to the Vase did not adversely affect its reputation – quite the contrary. As the new Museum construction was successfully completed, more and more visitors flowed in to view the treasures. When the British Museum first opened in the eighteenth century, visitors had only been allowed in small groups, which would be led around on an enforced guided tour. Now the floodgates were opened, and the hordes poured in, much to the distaste of Frederic Madden, Keeper of Manuscripts, no doubt. In 1851, two and a half million people visited the Museum, and a large proportion of them must have seen the restored Vase, now one of the most celebrated items in the collection.

As its fame spread among the culture-hungry Victorians, so the interpretations of the figures proliferated. Spinning theories about the frieze might have been a task specifically invented to enable a classically educated clergyman to fill up the long weekdays in his study at the rural deanery. During the second half of the nineteenth century, three more interpretations were published, and the pace was only just hotting up. After 1900, more interpretations would be devised and proclaimed than had appeared during the previous two and a half centuries.

In 1849 William Watkiss-Lloyd took up Winckelmann's earlier interpretation of the first scene as being the marriage of Peleus and Thetis. He was the first to draw attention to the verses in Catullus which embody the romantic, non-violent version of their courtship. The following year, a German scholar, C. T. Pyl, writing about the story of Medea, claimed the Vase for this myth. According to Pyl, figure F was Medea, and figure E was Jason. Medea had helped Jason to win the Golden Fleece; as the figure with the upended torch, she was perhaps mourning for the child she had dismembered and scattered on the waves in order to delay their pursuers when she fled with Jason from the palace of her father. But otherwise there does not seem to be the slightest evidence to support this theory.

But while the Vase grew in fame, open to the gaze of the

ever-growing hordes of visitors, its owner courted obscurity. To say that the Fifth Duke was a recluse is to put it mildly; in his endeavours to minimise his contact with the outside world he created a reputation for eccentricity which, without quite crossing the border into outright insanity, is unrivalled in all the annals of the crack-brained English aristocracy. John was not a lunatic; he never ran amok, flinging precious heirlooms right and left, convinced that he was Napoleon or that a Rosicrucian conspiracy had designs on his life. He does not appear ever to have lost his grip on reality. But this only makes his behaviour harder to account for; in all its long life the Vase never had an owner more *strange*.

The mother of John, Fifth Duke of Portland, showed signs of reclusiveness. She hid away from visitors to Welbeck, and even her servants learned to make themselves scarce when she approached, understanding that she did not like to be seen. It was perhaps at her behest that John was educated at home, but sooner or later he had to go out into the world, and he did; he joined the dragoon guards, and made a tall, good-looking cavalryman, with a reputation for fine horsemanship. He loved to hunt, and over the winter of 1820 to 1821 he went out with the hounds every single weekday, except when the frost was too hard. He travelled on the Continent, then fell for an opera-singer, Adelaide Kemble, daughter of the actor Charles, and proposed to her. Perhaps his affliction dates from her rejection; at about this time he began to complain of ill-health, sudden losses of memory, an irritation of the skin – things that could, perhaps, be put down to a 'nervous disposition', bearing in mind that John's constitution enabled him to reach the age of seventy-nine.

Gradually, he shrank from the world. Welbeck became his home and his castle, and he entrenched himself there, quite literally. He began to dig. First he dug the garden, laying out kitchen gardens over twenty-two acres, surrounded by high walls, with embrasures for braziers to warm and ripen the fruit. He built greenhouses, hothouses, and forcing-houses, for pineapples, peaches and grapes, but he had no company to eat them. He built an immense riding-house, more than a hundred metres long, lit by four thousand gas jets and a glass roof. Then he went underground: the Duke began to tunnel.

A tunnel was built from the house to the riding school, a thousand metres long, and wide enough for several people to walk abreast. Tunnels extended from the house to the park-gates, brick-lined, the width of two carriages. One, more than a mile long, led to the nearby town of Worksop. An underground chamber was excavated beside the house, a subterranean great hall, fifty metres long and painted pink. Armies of navvies, bricklayers, carpenters and plumbers were employed, with fleets of carts and traction-engines, and hundreds of thousands of pounds were spent on the works. John stipulated that the workers on the estate should be provided with donkeys to carry them from their encampment (known as 'Sligo' because of the nationality of those employed) to their work, and umbrellas to protect them from the weather. The Duke himself wore an exceedingly tall hat, and carried his own large umbrella as he watched the work, but employees were ordered to ignore him, not to address him or even acknowledge his presence. There is a story that one was dismissed for merely touching his hat to the Duke, but this seems out of character; the Duke appears to have been unfailingly kind and thoughtful in his own way, treating his staff with consideration, however misplaced, as he pursued his unfathomable schemes.

Inside the house he could shut himself up entirely. He communicated with the outside by a system of letter-boxes, two in each door, one for outgoing and the other for incoming messages. His were mostly addressed to his valet, who became his intermediary with the world. Boxes of clothes would be left outside the door, and plain, simple food brought in. John ate chicken, one a day – half at noon, and half for his evening meal. Under these circumstances it is hardly surprising that stories sprang up: the Duke was insane, suffering from a serious malady, hideously deformed, a Bluebeard, a syphilitic, a monster. But he was none of these things, and no such simple explanation can account for his behaviour. Certainly he was a hypochondriac, a recluse, and given the vast wealth he inherited with the dukedom, at liberty to indulge his whims. One of his own favourite phrases, oft-repeated in his letters, was 'Can anything be more absurd?' Absurd it certainly was – the wealthy aristocrat trundling down his broad tunnel in his equipage, past the hissing gas-lamps, but who knows what lonely melancholy brooded behind the thick curtains of his carriage, or why the Duke felt such an overwhelming need to go underground?

When John died he had, of course, no offspring, and the dukedom passed to a young male relative, who thus became the Sixth Duke. He had little idea what to expect when he came into his inheritance. His sister Ottoline, later Lady Ottoline Morrell, patroness of the Bloomsbury Group, but then a small child, described the scenes that met them when they arrived at Welbeck just before the Christmas of 1879. Welbeck was a building site, and they only reached the front door with the aid of planks laid across the workmen's rubble. Apart from the small apartment in which the Fifth Duke had lived, all the rooms were bare and painted pink, and empty of all furnishings and fittings except for a 'convenience' plumbed into the corner of each and not hidden in any way. The furniture was found piled in one large vaulted hall, and the pictures were stacked in the riding school, uncatalogued and without their frames. The Fifth Duke's apartment was filled with his collection of wigs, fine shirts and handkerchiefs. Tapestries were found and unrolled, cabinets were stumbled across, and in one Ottoline remembered her brother finding a secret drawer in which were hidden snuff-boxes, watches, miniatures and a green silk purse containing two thousand pounds' worth of banknotes.

So it is surely just as well that the Vase, safely ensconced in the

British Museum, escaped the consequences of the Fifth Duke's neglect; it might otherwise have been buried for ever in a mouldering heap of cabinets underground. Instead, shortly before the Fifth Duke died in solitude and seclusion, the fame of the Vase received a further boost at the hands of an individual, also called John, whose origins lay at the very opposite end of the social scale from the Vase's distinguished, eccentric owner.

Fifteenth Fragment
John Northwood

John Northwood was born in the 1830s, in a village on the road between Stourbridge and Wolverhampton. His father kept the village shop at the bottom of Glass House Hill; the name alerts us to the fact that this area of the English Midlands was a centre of glass manufacture, established by Huguenot refugees who settled there in the seventeenth century. Northwood was one of seven children, but only he and two brothers reached adulthood. He grew up in the 'Hungry Forties', a decade when, during the ruthless progress of the Industrial Revolution, famine and unemployment devastated the labouring classes. Despite the fact that his father sold groceries he knew what it was like to go short of food. He had no education, and was put to work at the age of twelve in Richardson's Glass Works, but immediately his great natural talents began to show themselves;

Northwood was not the kind of boy who would be left to sweep the floor. He learnt painting, gilding and enamelling. It became clear that he had a talent for drawing.

However able, Northwood was still at the bottom of the heap, and when the glass-works shut down temporarily, he was forced to go and work for his elder brother as a building labourer. He had to learn woodworking, exchanging the delicate brushes and tools of his trade for the saw and chisel. Perhaps he would have resigned himself to the life of a carpenter, a foot-soldier in the army of Victorian artisans, but Richardson's Works re-opened, and Northwood could go back to his first calling. Once again his talent marked him out. He learnt to paint on glass, and joined those paid piece-work rates for producing wares decorated in this fashion. Northwood was so much quicker than his older colleagues that he was forced to take a cut in his wages so as not to upset the natural order by earning more than his elders and betters.

At about this time, according to the son who dutifully recorded his life story, Northwood overheard his employer talking about the Portland Vase. Mr B. — or 'Uncle Ben' — Richardson had been thinking, as perhaps the proprietor of a glass-works might, about making a copy of the Portland Vase in glass. He had acquired one of the Wedgwood copies of the Vase, and brought it into the glass-works to show his craftsmen. 'There is a thousand pounds,' he announced, 'for him who can produce that in glass.' This challenge, as intended, fired Northwood's imagination, and stuck in his mind. Was it just the money? A young man with no education and little knowledge of the world, but an awareness of great ability, needs a goal. The Portland Vase became Northwood's.

Northwood was not the type to be held back by piece-rate work at Richardson's. By the time he was twenty-four Northwood had thought out a new way to etch decoration into glass using hydrofluoric acid. Glass could be coated with a layer of wax, the design could be drawn onto the surface with a steel point, and the piece next dipped in acid, which would then eat into the glass, following the marks of the design. If this sounds fairly straightforward, think for a moment how difficult it is to make a sharp point go where you want it to on the smooth, hard, curving surface of a piece of glassware. In Northwood's own understated words: 'it is an art of its own, and takes some considerable time and practice before one becomes sufficiently skilled to be able to make a correct and satisfactory pattern.'

Northwood set up in business for himself, with the help of one of the Richardson family, and his brother to do the books. They built a little factory with etching rooms, workshop and a plant for the difficult and dangerous business of manufacturing the acid. His son, who as a young apprentice must have taken part in this uncongenial business, describes in his book, *Crystal*, what it was like to work with the acid-bath:

In these days there were no fume extractors or ventilating fans and one had to have his acid-vat out in the open air, in bad weather under an open shed, and with no heating whatever the climate. The article could not be left in the bath of acid which was very strong, but had to be kept continually on the move. Our faces and hands used to suffer from the fumes. We had to keep removing the scum formed on the glass where acid was acting to prevent it eating down in an uneven way. To do this we had sticks of wood with a pad of cotton wool tied on the end which we called a 'mop'. The operation was to stand over the vat and whilst moving the article in the acid with one hand, we rubbed the mop over the surface of the glass with the other. So you see we could not get very far away from the fumes. It was always an unpleasant job and no-one wanted it.

The enterprise was a success, and Northwood became what a

contemporary might have described as a 'warm man' – someone to watch. Northwood refined his process and devised new ones; he invented an etching machine, which used a template to mark out the design mechanically, and he developed a technique that involved using a weak compound of the acid which only attacked the topmost surface of the glass, and could be used to create shading effects. The business flourished. For the first time in his life, Northwood had leisure, and he used it to visit London and see for himself the work of craftsmen who had gone before. He wandered through South Kensington and Bloomsbury, where the Victorians, with their burgeoning wealth and acquisitive energy, were busy piling up the treasures of the ages. He filled sketchbooks with what he saw, he gazed for the first time on the Vase itself and he felt thoroughly depressed. How could he hope to emulate the dazzling achievement of the ancient masters?

The parallels between John Northwood and Josiah Wedgwood hardly need to be pointed out, but this is perhaps the most telling similarity: like Wedgwood, when Northwood saw the Vase itself he was utterly crestfallen. Is this the usual reaction of the visitor to the British Museum? Do we go round in a haze of disappointment and dismay because we ourselves don't have it in us to come up with something like the Elgin Marbles or the Lewis Chessmen? Both Northwood and Wedgwood harboured genuine, vaulting ambition; they hoped they could try to emulate the ancient masters, and once confronted by the masterworks themselves, by the appalling difficulty of the task, with that hope came despair. But they also both possessed near superhuman amounts of dedication, energy and courage that enabled them to put so much time and effort into fine work on fragile objects.

The Elgin Marbles became the inspiration for Northwood's first conscious attempt to produce a masterpiece of glass-carving. He embarked on the decoration of a large glass vase which he called the

'Elgin Vase', because it was to be decorated with figures copied from the Marbles. Granted, he had a successful business to run, and could only work on the project in his spare time, but it took him *nine years*; nine years of snatched moments represent an awesome amount of concentration on one fragile piece. There were accidents; at one point he dropped his carving tool on the foot of the vase, and it was some time before he could bring himself to look down and see if he had broken the glass – he hadn't. Then, when he was carving the handle of the vase, the point of his tool broke off in the junction between the handle and the body, and after several days of struggling to get it out, he was forced to remove it by carefully dissolving it with acid.

Northwood finished his Elgin Vase in 1873. It could claim to be the most successful piece of carved glass in the modern age; the *Worcestershire Daily Gazette* recklessly asserted that it was the most important work of its kind since the Roman era. But as far as Northwood was concerned, it was just a trial piece. The Elgin Vase was carved in clear, transparent glass; the Portland Vase was another matter.

First the blank – the basic uncarved body of glass – had to be produced. Philip Pargeter, Richardson's nephew and a friend and colleague of Northwood, volunteered to make the attempt, and also offered to put up the cash prize once promised by his uncle. 'We had failures, as might have been expected, and I had to be very firm with the men,' remarks Pargeter, showing the authentic Victorian attitude to labour relations. Northwood's son described the process Pargeter followed, in the 1924 *Journal of the Society of Glass Technology*. First, a 'cup-shaped article of opal white glass' was produced. 'This cup, while in the hot state, is completely filled up solid with molten, transparent, coloured glass gathered on the end of a glass blowing iron.' This was then rolled on an iron plate, called a 'marver', in order to weld the two different glasses – the white and the blue –

together. It was then reheated in the furnace, to keep it 'in a soft and ductile state for the glass-blower to blow the solid mass into a hollow-shaped ball. The finisher or workman takes charge of it at this stage, and by his skilful manipulation forms it into the shape and size of the article desired.' It was then 'annealed' – gradually cooled from its hot state by being placed in an oven. This description gives us a very clear idea of how the Vase itself may have been produced.

Having successfully produced a workable blank, Pargeter handed it over to Northwood so that he could begin his epic task. As a humble artisan Northwood wasn't at first allowed any special access to the Vase – he could only peer at it as it sat in its display case in the British Museum. He noticed that the white glass that formed the outer layer of the Vase only reached up to its shoulder; it did not cover the neck. This meant that while the lower end of the handles rested on white glass, the upper end rested on blue. From the viewpoint of a glass-worker he speculated about the reasons for this: when the blue glass was dipped in white, was there not sufficient white glass to cover the whole piece? Or did the ancient craftsman deliberately leave the neck uncovered in order to lessen the strain created by the tiny differences in expansion of the two layers of glass?

Northwood knew from practical experience that expansion is the major difficulty in producing a piece from two different layers of glass, that when the glass is taken from the furnace it is at its highest expansion, and as it cools it contracts. Different layers will inevitably contract at different rates and by different degrees; a state of tension could be set up within the vase. This tension might not show itself at once; it could lurk invisibly, waiting for some trigger to release it. That Northwood knew all this did not necessarily mean he could defend himself from his own catastrophe.

Northwood's first step was in a way to cheat; he drew the design onto the outer, white layer, painted over it with a varnish made from bitumen, and dipped the piece in his acid-bath, using his own process to give himself a flying start. The acid removed the white glass from around where the figures would be, letting large areas of blue show through, thus saving a great deal of work. But once this basic step had been taken, he had to begin carving.

This exceedingly practical experiment is perhaps the best opportunity we have of understanding how the original Vase was carved. Northwood's equipment was home-made and simple in the extreme. His carving tool was a finely tempered steel rod, sharpened to a point, and held in a wooden surround, like a pencil. As he worked he dipped the point in paraffin to cool it and give it bite. As time went on he developed a device which resembled a propelling pencil, with jaws on the wooden handle that allowed the rod to be fed through as the point wore away. The point was sharpened by rubbing on an oilstone. He rested the glass on a pad made of moleskin, filled with bran. Northwood worked long hours, and he must have felt an enormous amount of pressure. To say that he needed to concentrate is something of an understatement: he could not afford to make a single false step. Once the glass was carved away it could not be put back, so any glass removed in the wrong place would destroy the work. If he had been working on an original design, a mistake of this nature could perhaps have been incorporated into it, and no one would have been the wiser. But copying the Vase removed even this recourse, and made the task that much harder.

He had a small room built within the larger workshop, partitioned off to protect him from the noise and bustle, and worked away steadily for several years. As he worked he constantly studied the Vase, both the original and a Wedgwood copy. He had no access to photographic equipment and he could not, like Wedgwood, take the Vase back to his workshop and gloat over it. He had nothing but the skill of his own hand and eye. He had to rely on his own sketches, made during repeated visits to the British Museum. Sometimes he would take his vase with him to London, so that he could compare his work-in-progress with the finished article. A special wooden box was made by Edwin Grice, one of Northwood's craftsmen, then lined with velvet, and set up so that the work fitted perfectly into it. Even so, how nerve-racking such a trip must have been for Northwood, jolting over the rail-lines into Euston Station, and threading the busy streets of the capital with his precious burden. He made careful drawings of the different figures in the frieze, and when he returned to his workshop he would set to work while the sight of the original was fresh in his mind. During daylight hours he worked on the smaller, more detailed parts; when it grew dark he would carve by the light of the largest, most powerful oil-lamps, passing the rays of the lamp through a globe of water to focus the light.

Northwood had become something of a celebrity, his ambitious projects stimulating the public imagination like the record-breaking attempts of athletes or yachtsmen. The works-yard would fill up with the carriages of visitors come to view the sport, and so Northwood had to contend not only with the difficulties and dangers of his work, but also with the gentry breathing down his neck and asking asinine questions. The press published bulletins of the progress of the work, and this would make it all the more humiliating when disaster struck – which it did, at the very last moment. After several years, his copy was nearly finished. Northwood decided to take it to London to compare it one last time with the original, and confirm that it was as perfect as he could make it. The Museum had given him permission to take the Portland Vase itself out of its case in order to measure it and compare it with the nearly completed copy. According to one account, before he went, he decided to wash his vase in warm water, and this simple act triggered the disaster. But Edwin Grice told a different story to the *Stourbridge County Express*:

Before we started early for London we had a terrible mishap. The night had been very frosty, and when the vase was being lifted carefully into the box something went crack. We afterwards found that the holding of the vase in warm hands had caused uneven expansion, producing a fracture. It put a damper on our spirits, as you may guess.

As Northwood had carved away at the white, outer layer, the tensions within the vase, set up by the initial cooling process, had changed. Now the vase was more sensitive to a change in temperature – any change that would affect the existing tension. The crack ran right up the body of the vase. Imagination must supply Northwood's feelings.

Close examination of the Portland Vase itself reveals that it has been ground *on the inside*. Tiny horizontal lines run around the inside of the Vase, and these were almost certainly made during its manufacture, but for what purpose? Perhaps the grinding was undertaken to thin the walls of the Vase and make the dark-blue glass more translucent, but no such effect has been achieved; indeed, the blue glass is almost opaque. Only if you bend down and look up so that your gaze passes through the shoulder of the Vase and out of the mouth – in other words through only one wall of glass – can you detect any transparency at all. It is also fairly obvious that very little glass was removed by this grinding. An alternative explanation has been suggested by two modern glass experts, William Gudenrath and David Whitehouse. They developed the hypothesis that the grinding was related to the tensions set up within the Vase; if there was stress between the inner and outer layers of the Vase, this would exhibit itself most powerfully on the inner surface. Gudenrath and Whitehouse went so far as to demonstrate this theory by blowing a glass vessel, and then, instead of cooling it gently in an annealing furnace, plunging it straight into cold water. This savage cooling set up tensions within the vessel. They still managed to grind the outside without producing any ill effects, but when they only gently abraded the inside, the vessel shattered. Their conclusion was that the Vase was subjected to the internal grinding process before work began on the carving, in an attempt to discover and alleviate any internal stresses. There is no evidence that Northwood knew of or followed this technique, and it may have led to his downfall. It seems that the original makers of the Vase displayed more technical expertise than their Victorian successor.

Northwood's actions were phlegmatic enough, however. He stuck the pieces back together and carried on. Grice described how the vase was glued: 'We strapped the vase round with rubber bands and other things, put it on the boiler side for a fortnight to keep it warm, and at the expiration of that time it took a very sharp eye to detect that it had been cracked at all.' The vase was 'finished', the evidence of the disaster covered over as well as it could be, the commission fulfilled to the apparent satisfaction of all concerned. If Northwood's copy had flaws, these after all only brought it into closer sympathy with the original, now webbed with cracks. Indeed, Northwood's vase was displayed to great acclaim, and single-handedly inspired a sudden demand for cameo glass. Manufactories rushed to fulfil the desires of their customers for such costly novelties, and a furious revival of cameo glass took place in late-Victorian England, creating a whole new industry. For another fifty years, Northwood and his descendants and rivals catered for the taste that his copy of the Portland Vase had stimulated. Oddly enough, the craze disappeared as quickly as it had arisen, because of either the decline in the economic fortunes of the leisured classes or a change in taste, or perhaps both. In this respect, the late-Victorian craze for cameo glass may have mirrored the original burst of such creativity under the Caesars, which seems to have been similarly short-lived.

The fame of the Vase continued to grow, and theories about its figures to proliferate. In 1879, as the Vase passed from the ownership of the Fifth to the Sixth Duke of Portland, another scholar, W. Klein, connected the Vase with a story about Theseus, which involves the hero making a journey beneath the sea to retrieve the ring of King Minos from Neptune. Klein proposed that the first side of the Vase is actually an underwater scene. Figure A is Theseus, figure C is the sea-goddess Amphitrite, and D is Neptune. The tree that grows between these two figures is perhaps a sturdy frond of seaweed, and Cupid is not flying, but swimming through the water, his torch burning magically without air. But the theories made no difference to the Vase's popularity. Copies of it were made and sold by the Museum in such numbers that by the beginning of the twentieth century the Keeper of Greek and Roman Antiquities was complaining that the mould they used was becoming too worn. Its physical form restored, its reputation enhanced to notoriety by its adventures, the Vase was a famous highlight of and fixture in the British Museum. But in 1929, greatly to the surprise of the trustees responsible for it, it became apparent that the Vase was about to set out on its travels again.

Sixteenth Fragment
Christie's

In 1929 the Vase was put up for sale by the Sixth Duke of Portland, apparently without any consultation with its guardians at the Museum, but of course there was nothing they could do to stop him. The Director of the Museum, Sir Frederic Kenyon (who was the grandson of Edward Hawkins, the Keeper of Antiquities responsible for prosecuting William Mulcahy), wrote a letter to the trustees of the Museum, alerting them 'that announcements have appeared in the press of the sale at Christie's on May 2nd of the Portland Vase'. Kenyon was referring to a news item in the *Times* printed on 7 March, which quoted from the catalogue for the sale: 'Messrs Christie announce that they will sell at their rooms, 8, King-street, St James's-square, on May 2nd, "the world famous and historic vase of antique glass" known as the Portland or Barberini Vase.'

The *Times* reminded its readers that the Vase was 'not a national possession, but merely on loan to the British Museum'. It hinted that it had, unlike the trustees, some prior knowledge of the sale: 'It was known some months ago that the sale of the Portland Vase was within the range of possibilities.' It speculated excitedly about the sum that the Vase might fetch: 'The word "priceless" is often carelessly applied to pictures and other objects of art. But we may well ask what is this, one of the greatest and most beautiful specimens of ancient art, going to fetch under the hammer?' The *Times* refrained from making its own estimate. Instead, ever the champion of the haves over the have-nots, it stoutly defended in its editorial the Duke's decision to sell what after all was his own property: 'There will be sore hearts to-day among the lovers of the beautiful ... Even so, grief may justly be tempered with gratitude; for it is much that successive generations have been able to see and admire the vase.' The Thunderer went further: it was in fact the fault of the common people that the Vase was to be sold, as the Duke,

it can be safely assumed, has been driven to reclaim his possession only by pressure at the hands of the same public which has up to now enjoyed it as if it had been its own ... Necessary as high taxation may be, the nation cannot expect to be able to impose it in increasing doses and indefinitely to enjoy favours from the victims. The disappearance of the vase from its familiar pedestal is bound to alarm the conscientious who keep their eyes open. There are pictures in public galleries of a tenure equally precarious; and outside the world of art there are many privileges of access and usufruct which the public is apt unthinkingly to regard as perpetual.

So hands off our aristocracy, or you'll regret it!

The reappearance of the Vase in the news was enough to stimulate the mind of Professor Frank S. Granger, of University College Nottingham, who wrote a long letter to Christie's three weeks after the initial announcement of the sale, containing yet another interpretation of the figures on the Vase, the first to make it into print in the twentieth century. Professor Granger, braving the displeasure of Henry Stuart-Jones, reasserted the connection with Alexander Severus, but with a Neoplatonic twist. In his interpretation Figure C is Mammaea, the mother of Alexander Severus, and figure A is Alexander the Great. So here Alexander the Great assists at or inspires the birth of the Emperor; this accords with the very first theory considered, which was put forward by Girolamo Teti way back in 1642. On the other side, figure F, the female figure reclining with upended torch, is Mammaea again, and figure G, Professor Granger decided, is one of the Fates. The three Fates sat beside Pluto in the underworld: Clotho spun the thread of life from her spindle of raw wool, Lachesis twisted it to make it stronger or weaker and Atropos sat ready with the shears to cut it off at the appointed time. Granger suggests that Figure G is Clotho, and the staff she holds is the spindle from which the thread of Mammaea's life is wound. The frieze as a whole, therefore, serves to commemorate the life and death of Mammaea.

Like some of his predecessors, Granger does not seem to have been willing or able to look closely at the Vase. He suggests that the square block lying at Mammaea's feet 'may, perhaps, be a book'. He is more certain about the figure on the base of the Vase; this is 'probably Orpheus on his mysterious errand, the descent into hell. Him an imaginative reader might well identify with Christ' (who also went down to hell after his crucifixion, to release the souls kept there since the Fall). Granger thus detects a theme – Birth on the first side, Death on the second, and Immortality on the base. Alexander Severus, he asserts, showed such tolerance to the early Christian Church that 'it is possible to regard their joint rule ... as the first Christian

Government known to the world'. The Emperor himself seems to have had leanings – Christian images were found in the imperial chapel. So to Granger the figures on the Vase can be approached 'in the light of early Christian art combined as it so often is with the use of classical symbols'. Having dragged in an entire new iconography, however, Granger meekly retires: 'These suggestions are made with no claim to certainty; but in the light of the whole circumstances of the Vase, they seem to me exceedingly probable.'

At the beginning of April a letter arrived from the Duke's solicitors, Baileys, Shaw and Gillett, asking the trustees to hand the Vase over to Christie's 'at 10.30 am on Wednesday, 17th April'. The Duke wrote personally to Frederic Kenyon 'to say how very deeply and sincerely I regret to be obliged to sell the "Portland Vase" owing to the exigencies of the present times'. The Duke recorded the 'pleasure and satisfaction' that the loan to the Museum had given him. He offered 'an expression of my gratitude to you and the Trustees for the care they have so long taken of my Family property'. This statement seems to have been made without irony, despite the fact that when his ancestor had first lent the Vase to the Museum it had been in one piece, and now was in about two hundred, albeit glued together. The Duke even repetitiously expressed 'my regret to you, to the Trustees, and to the Public in general that I am obliged to come to this regrettable decision'.

Kenyon's reply was equally formal and fulsome; he informed the Duke that 'the Trustees will appreciate highly your kind words with regard to them, and to the long period during which they have been custodians of this remarkable monument of ancient craftsmanship', and thus tacitly thanked the Duke for overlooking the regrettable incident involving the Irish student and the lump of basalt. Kenyon reassured the Duke that the trustees 'have never doubted that it is only with the greatest reluctance that you have decided to withdraw the Vase from the Museum, and to offer it for sale by public auction.

Naturally they share your regret, but they recognise the decision is one they cannot question.'

This correspondence was published in the *Morning Post* of 10 April, under an extensive and eye-catching headline:

PORTLAND VASE SALE
DUKE OF PORTLAND'S DEEP REGRET
LETTER TO MUSEUM DIRECTOR
SIR F. KENYON AND AUCTION ROOM
COMPETITION

The last two lines of this refer to a muted cry for help which Kenyon made in the knowledge that the correspondence would be published: 'If means could be found for preserving this famous work of Art for the Museum, I need hardly say that the Trustees would gratefully welcome it; but they have no available resources at their own disposal to meet the competition of the auction-room.' But no rich benefactor stepped forward with an open cheque-book, and the fateful day arrived when the Vase had to leave the Museum.

In all the Vase's wanderings, the trip it made from the British Museum in Bloomsbury to Christie's auction house in King Street – a journey that one can make on foot in twenty minutes – must be one of the shortest it ever took, but it is by far the best documented. Two London papers, the *Morning Post* and the *Evening News*, both devoted extensive column inches to the event; unconcerned with the limp-wristed gestures of the League of Nations, or the parlous state of the German economy, they were utterly fascinated by the local movement of the Vase, in a style inescapably reminiscent of Evelyn Waugh. The *Morning Post* was the more upmarket of the two newspapers, and its correspondent actually accompanied into the Museum the man sent by Christie's to fetch the Vase, 'Mr T Rogers, of Mason's Yard, who for upwards of forty years has been employed by Messrs Christie's for the packing and transport of priceless works of art'. The *Morning Post* saw Rogers's specially prepared packing case, which was taken to Kenyon's office, where the Vase was now waiting. The Vase was already packed inside a smaller case 'which had been especially constructed for the safety of the Vase during the war'. This case was opened for Rogers's examination, and then the smaller case was carefully lowered into the larger. While this was going on, the Secretary of the Museum and the Keeper of Antiquities chatted confidentially to the *Post*, voicing their regret at the Vase's loss, and 'the slight hope that it may be purchased by some patriotic Englishman, who will lend it once more to the nation'.

The correspondent of the *Evening News*, an organ altogether closer to the gutter, was not offered the opportunity to hobnob with the high-ups; he was kept out on the street, with the crowd. But as befitted his station by the kerb, his style was rather punchier. A melodramatic headline set the tone: 'PORTLAND VASE IN A PLAIN VAN – Hush-Hush Departure from the British Museum – MYSTERY.' The reporter staked out the Museum and quizzed the warders, who 'flatly stated that it had been removed shortly before 10 o'clock. But this statement lacked conviction, since I had been watching the courtyard of the British Museum since half past nine. I had not seen anything like a packing case carried out.' Eventually, having penetrated as far as the entrance to the Gold Room, which was now roped off from the general public, the watchful eye of the *Evening News* was rewarded:

Suddenly there was a quick patter of feet, and round the corner from the private offices of the Graeco-Roman antiquity department, a man came hurrying, swinging in his hand what looked like a big leather-covered box with a strap handle. He scurried across the room in which the crowd had gathered; a panel slid aside in the further corner of the room; he vanished

[196]

through the opening; the panel slammed after him and that was that.

The *Evening News* reporter then renewed his vigil in the courtyard, which was eventually rewarded by a sight of the Vase, now repacked in Mr Rogers's wooden case, 'with a light padlock', being carried down the steps to a waiting van. 'We all held our breath, while two men lifted it into the back of a plain green van, and settled it comfortably in the corner. One of the old men in charge' – presumably Mr Rogers himself – 'seated himself – yes he actually seated himself – on the box containing the Portland Vase, lit a pipe, and was driven away.'

The indefatigable reporter flagged down a taxi – 'Follow that Vase!' – and gave chase as the van drove down Great Russell Street and then on to Shaftesbury Avenue. He confessed himself thrilled at the thought of the priceless object weaving its way through the Wednesday morning traffic 'with all the crowds of ordinary Londoners going unconsciously about their business all round it. The aged retainer sat on his box and smoked imperturbably the whole way.' But then no one seemed to be quite as excited by the proceedings as the newshound himself. The Vase reached Christie's, unmolested by armed gangs or car-smashes, and was conveyed down into the strongroom, where it awaited the day of the sale.

The auction took place on 2 May, and drew one of the biggest crowds ever seen at Christie's. Members of the public queued for hours, armed with lunchboxes. Photographers swarmed through the throng. The bidding was started at ten thousand pounds, and went up by the thousand. Two or three bidders ran the total up to nearly thirty thousand pounds. But this was apparently well below the reserve placed on it by the Duke. The *Morning Post* had not sullied its pages with vulgar speculation about how much the Vase might fetch, but the *Evening News* had not been so restrained. 'Anything between £50,000 and £100,000' was their guess, and the lower figure may not have been so wide of the mark, at least as far as the Duke was concerned. Thirty thousand was certainly not enough for him. The auctioneer 'bought in' by making a bid himself. The whole anti-climactic process only took a couple of minutes, and some in the crowd were not aware of what had happened; a female voice cried, 'The British public demands to know who has bought it!' But no one had bought it. The auctioneer's bid remained, and no one was prepared to go any higher.

The Duke, not prepared to sell the Vase for as little as thirty thousand pounds, took it back into his own keeping, where it remained for the next three years. If during this time he intended or actually attempted to find a buyer prepared to pay a price he considered worthy, he met with no success. The 'exigencies' which had prompted him to try to sell the Vase were not so pressing that he was prepared to settle for less, and by 1932, it seems they were pressing more gently on the ducal finances. The Duke wrote to the trustees, offering to renew the loan on condition that he could take the vase and sell it whenever he chose. They, having paused to consider whether they needed to renew their stock of postcards of the Vase, then out of print, gratefully accepted. In April 1932, almost three years to the day since the Vase had left the Museum, it was handed back to the Keeper of Greek and Roman Antiquities, and placed on view in the same position in which it had stood before the auction. Perhaps this was a homecoming, and perhaps the Vase itself might have hoped that a peaceful existence now lay before it, but if so its hopes would soon be dashed. Only a few years later, the Vase was in the process of acquiring a new owner, bombshells – real and high-explosive rather than metaphorical – were raining down on the British Museum, and, under very different circumstances, the Vase was once again to be smashed into hundreds of pieces.

Seventeenth Fragment

Restoration

In September 1940, during the beginnings of the Blitz, two bombs fell on the British Museum. They fell in almost exactly the same spot, the second coming through the hole made by the first, and both failed to explode. Fate seemed to be looking after the Museum. In October an incendiary landed on the roof of the Round Reading Room, in the centre of the building, but the interior did not catch, and the blaze was extinguished. Then one night in May 1941, at the height of the bombing, the Museum's luck ran out. Seven hundred tons of bombs were dropped on central London in the course of the night of 10 May, and thousands of fires started. The Museum was hit by a stick of incendiaries; some of them penetrated to the attic space between the copper roof and the plaster ceilings, and this time the fire took hold, doing immense damage before it was brought under control by the firefighters. A whole range of galleries on the south-west side of the building was lost. The Museum building then housed collections belonging to the British Library, and one hundred and fifty thousand books were destroyed, some by flames, some by water. Researchers in the British Library today may still be informed that the book they have found in the catalogue is unavailable, having been 'destroyed by enemy action'.

The first-floor gallery which houses the Greek and Roman collection today was left a blackened shell, open to the sky. Its floor was sealed to protect the galleries below, and after a while rainwater produced a large internal lake, across which stepping-stones were laid to allow the staff to traverse what was left of the room.

The Vase fortunately escaped the inferno. It had been removed, along with the rest of the treasures of the Museum, for safekeeping outside the capital. But unlike those of its crated companions in exile, the Vase's fate was still uncertain. In 1943 the Sixth Duke of Portland died, and a year later the Seventh Duke let it be known that he was also minded to sell the Vase. The trustees decided that they might dare to enquire the price. For some time nothing was done; the fight for national survival was something of a distraction, and the Keeper of Antiquities himself, Bernard Ashmole, was on war service. But Ashmole's stand-in, a Mr Allen, made a strong case for purchase in a report to the trustees, based firmly on the fame of the Vase. He pointed out that the Museum and the Vase were inseparably associated in the mind of the general public, and that the Vase's notoriety gave it a special value. The taxpayer would not mind paying for something that had become a national treasure and an object of fascination.

In 1944 the Seventh Duke revealed that he would part with the Vase for as little as five thousand pounds. Compared to the sums bandied around at the Christie's sale, this was surely a bargain. The Museum made an offer, finding the money in a timely bequest, but another year went by and the war in Europe was dragging to its close before the Duke replied to accept. On the day before Armistice Day, a formal receipt was issued to the Duke, and the Vase was the property of the Museum. It had changed hands for the last time.

Now the Vase was finally in the keeping of the Museum, or at least it was so assumed, but an unusual donation revealed that not *all* of it was. Unknown to those responsible for it, part of the Vase had been wandering in the wilderness for a hundred years. In 1948, Bernard Ashmole, now safely returned from the war, received a box containing thirty-seven tiny chips of glass. They had been brought in by a Mr Crocker of Putney, who didn't know what they were, but thought the Museum might be able to identify them. The Museum could: they were splinters from the Portland Vase. What the Museum couldn't at first understand was what on earth they were doing in the possession of Mr Crocker, but gradually the story was untangled.

The glass splinters were Doubleday's leavings, pieces for which he had been unable to find a place in his reconstruction of 1845. When Doubleday died, a colleague had taken these fragments to a Mr G. H. Gabb, a box-maker, so that a suitable container could be constructed with little compartments to hold the splinters. This colleague then also died, and it seems that the commission died with him. Gabb duly made the box, in which he placed the splinters, but simply forgot to return it. Decades passed, Gabb himself died, and his executrix, a Miss Reeves, found the box among his effects. She passed it on to Crocker; he took it into the Museum.

To Ashmole the fragments represented an opportunity: why not restore the Vase again? Doubleday's work was a hundred years old, and the glue he had used was decaying and discoloured and had become unsightly; the cracks were literally showing. Techniques had improved over the last century, and now the Museum's restorers could make a better job of it. Ashmole also admitted to curiosity; he wanted to know whether the base of the Vase really belonged to it or not, and restoration would give him a chance to find out. In November 1948 one of the Museum's restorers, J. H. W. Axtell, was given the task. But first of course he had to take it to pieces. Doubleday's glue was removed, and once again the Vase was reduced to fragments, laid out in an intimidating jigsaw. The event was witnessed by Ashmole and assembled experts, who were invited to handle the pieces. One of them recorded his excitement at this historic experience, as reported in the 1990 *Journal of Glass Studies*:

> This seemed an occasion unlikely to recur, like the seeing of the King's College windows at inches distant on the ground. As some of the fragments passed, amid guarded silences, through my fingers, there came into my head the title of the Ambrose Bierce collection *Can Such Things Be?*

The freshly restored Vase was back on show by spring of the following year, and all agreed it looked much improved. Ashmole established to his own satisfaction that the base disc did not belong to the Vase originally, but was a later addition, though how much later was not certain. But the splinters themselves proved a disappointment. In the event, Axtell had only found a place for three of them, and the rest continued their exile, left to languish in the box made by Mr Gabb.

The Vase may now have been restored and secured, but controversy surrounding the interpretation of its figures did not abate. New theories sprang up like dragon's teeth, thick and fast and somewhat fantastical. Study of the Vase involved an ever more dizzying whistle-stop tour through the major events of Greek mythology. In 1964 D. E. L. Haynes restated the Peleus and Thetis argument, but perversely insisted that Figure C was not Thetis, but her mother, or even her grandmother. In 1965 H. Mobius joined the Theseus-at-the-bottom-of-the-sea clique, with the added insight that

Figure F was Ariadne, lying disconsolately on the isle of Naxos. Ariadne, daughter of Minos, slips Theseus the ball of thread by which he makes his way through the Labyrinth, and thus helps him defeat her father's monster the Minotaur, but she is then abandoned by the ungrateful hero on Naxos. In 1966 F. L. Bastet came out in support of this theory, but insisted that the whole frieze referred to the story of Theseus and Ariadne, and that figure C was Ariadne as well. In 1967 Bernard Ashmole himself weighed in with his own theory, which for its combination of detailed study, impressive weight of knowledge and slight battiness, is well worth examining in greater detail.

Ashmole brought to the task not just the fruit of a lifetime's study of antiquities: he had had ample opportunity during his tenure as Keeper of Antiquities to examine the Vase. He had also been present during its restoration, and had handled the separate pieces, along with his awe-struck colleagues. This certainly put him a cut above those who were not even able to identify the gender of some of the figures correctly. He began his account by making the very sensible observation that whoever created the Vase, having necessarily lavished a great deal of time and effort on it, was quite likely to have given some thought to the figures being depicted, and would have chosen the subject and its conveyed meaning carefully. He made another important point, that the Romans were in the habit of using subjects of Greek mythology to convey more than one meaning; the scenes from Greek mythology that decorate the sides of many Roman sarcophagi – including the one in which the Vase itself was supposed to have been found – were not there by chance, but because the Romans considered the stories these scenes illustrated to be allegories of the afterlife. Sometimes portraits of those for whom the sarcophagi were intended were superimposed on the bodies of the gods and heroes. The intended meaning of the figures on the Vase, then, might be highly esoteric. Knowledge needed to decode this meaning may have belonged to the 'initiated', and as this knowledge was lost, so any interpretation of the Vase might now be impossible. This was a brave attempt to swim against the current; one thing Ashmole's predecessors had in common was a belief that the Vase could be decoded – by them. But of course Ashmole himself then immediately set this consideration aside, in his own attempt to provide an interpretation.

Ashmole started with Side I and the Peleus and Thetis myth, and he heartily endorsed this theory. To him the identification of Figure C as the sea-nymph Thetis with her sea-serpent, and of Figure A, reaching out to her but looking anxiously over her head at Figure D, and Figure D himself, brooding over the union being effected in front of him, perfectly fitted the story outlined above: it showed Neptune's desire for Thetis giving way to the dangerous prophecy, and grudging permission being given for her marriage to the mortal Peleus. Ashmole strengthened this interpretation by reassessing the masks below the handles. According to many previous scholars, these are of Pan, thus identified because of his goat-horns. But close examination of the masks reveals that these horns are an illusion; they are simply strips of uncarved white glass running round the join between the handle and the Vase. The masks do not have horns, and they do have fleshy, fish-like lips. They are, maintained Ashmole, the face of the God Oceanus, grandfather of Thetis. Oceanus was the fount of life; on his stream, so the Romans believed, the souls of the dead were carried to the next life, and his face is commonly seen on Roman sarcophagi. Ashmole's interpretation of Side I of the Vase is highly convincing, perhaps the most convincing of all those yet proffered, combining as it does the strongest elements of previous interpretations together with fresh insight. The story fits the picture; the relationships of the figures, the action, their attributes are all accounted for. However, Ashmole's stab at the second side of the Vase is altogether wilder.

In interpreting this side, Ashmole focuses on the reclining female figure, and specifically on her breasts. He admires these enthusiastically – more than just cold ink runs in this scholar's veins – but his admiration does not stem merely from personal predilection. These magnificent assets are a give-away, an identifying feature that can belong to none other than Helen of Troy, the Marilyn Monroe of Greek myth. Ashmole quotes chapter and verse on Helen's breasts from the highest authorities. According to the myth, when Troy falls, and Menelaus, Helen's husband, discovers his runaway wife and gives chase in a vengeful fury, Venus intervenes to save her merely by arranging for her disordered dress to reveal her breasts as she flees. A character in Aristophanes' play *Lysistrata* mentions the incident: 'Menelaus, when he somehow saw the breasts of Helen naked, threw away the sword I think.' The mere sight of her charms was enough utterly and abruptly to quench ten years of bloody, brooding anger. This central figure then, is Helen, and the figure on her left, Figure E, is Achilles, with whom, according to one version of the myth, Helen ended up in the Isles of the Blessed, feasting and drinking in the afterlife. Achilles, greatest of all Greek heroes, was the offspring of Peleus and Thetis, and his union with Helen after death brings to a close the whole history of the Trojan War. The two sides of the Vase are thus related: they show the beginning and end of the entire saga. Figure G, Ashmole maintains, is the goddess Venus, who presides over so many events in that story. The identification of Achilles is, to Ashmole, confirmed by the pillar beside him; this is his grave stele, or marker. Ashmole's theory is interesting, but it fails to deal with the torch that figure F is holding. This torch may symbolise death, but it hardly accords with the blissful afterlife implied by the myth. Nor, logically, should Achilles be sitting by his grave, if he has been magically transported elsewhere to enjoy the company of the beautiful Helen.

Over the next twenty years nine more theories were published, more than even this exhaustive work cares to elaborate. Writers began to find it increasingly necessary to deal with their predecessors' theories first, setting out their position in the continuing debate – 'I partly agree with *x* but not *y*' – before going on to make their own diagnosis, which would often be merely a recombination or reconfiguration of two or more previous attempts. Many agreed that figure C was Thetis, although one introduced yet another set of mythical characters by deciding that figure C was actually Andromeda, who is presented as a sacrifice by her parents to the sea-monster then ravaging their kingdom, and rescued by Perseus. According to this theory Figure A is Perseus, and the sea-monster is rearing its ugly though rather diminutive head between Andromeda's legs. Interpretations of Side II varied still more widely. Iphigenia and Augustus's daughter Julia were both suggested for the role. At the end of the 1970s John Hind, happy to accept the Peleus-and-Thetis theory for Side I, came up with another entirely new and perfectly plausible explanation for Side II. Hind remarked that in order to stand up, any interpretation ought to account for all the obvious attributes of all the figures. This is a very sensible point, and Hind does his best to adhere to it by referring to the story of Aeneas and Dido.

Fleeing Troy after its destruction at the end of the Trojan War, Aeneas arrives in Carthage, a city still being built at the behest of its beautiful and widowed queen, Dido. Dido falls in love with the Trojan prince, and, according to a famous passage in Virgil's *Aeneid*, they consummate their love in a cave in the forest, having been forced to take shelter from a storm while out hunting. Unfortunately, Aeneas's fate lies elsewhere; his destiny is the foundation of Rome, and he has no choice but to leave Dido, who in her despair commits suicide, throwing herself on her own funeral pyre. Hind detects something restless in the seated pose of figure E: the bent leg and slight angle of the torso suggest to him that this figure is on the point of rising, that is, going away and thus deserting figure F. Figure E is

Aeneas, and figure F, then, is Dido, reclining in despair, the torch that symbolises both her burning love and her self-lit funeral pyre hanging from her fingers. Above them arch the trees of the forest, and below them are the rocks, together representing the forest grotto where the lovers lie together. Figure G is Venus, who presides over the fate of Aeneas, and who sternly bids him leave the fleshpots of Carthage in order to fulfil his destiny. To Hind the theme is war: while on Side I the marriage of Peleus and Thetis sets in train events which will lead to the Trojan War, Side II commemorates the symbolic beginning of the Carthaginian Wars, during which the youthful Roman Republic and the sea-power of Carthage fought to the death for control of the Mediterranean.

After Hind, during the 1980s, as word-processors proliferated and the comfortable lifestyles of academics allowed them yet more leisure time for the consideration of these abstruse matters, at least four more theories were published, involving in various combinations Theseus, Apollo, Perseus, Achilles, Augustus, Romulus, Atia, Andromeda, Thetis, Iphigenia, Julia and so on, and so on. Meanwhile, as the decade drew to a close, while the controversy continued unabated, and the scholars dissected each other's hypotheses, the Vase itself was once again pulled apart.

*

In 1985 a new Roman Gallery was being prepared at the British Museum, and in this the Portland Vase was, of course, to be the lead attraction. Prior to the opening of this new gallery the Vase was inspected by the Museum's conservators, and found to be in poor shape. Either the Department of Conservation had grown harder to please, or the work of the 1940s was not holding up as well as Doubleday's earlier effort. Less than forty years after Axtell had made his restoration, the adhesive he had used was yellowing and brittle, and the filling shrunk and disfigured. The conservators put the Vase under the microscope. This revealed that Axtell had added a blue pigment to his adhesive in order to hide the joins, but this pigment had a weakening effect. In some places the adhesive was starting to fall out. A less technical experiment was also undertaken: tapping the Vase – gently – with a fingernail did not produce the ringing sound associated with a happily cohering vessel. Nigel Williams, head of the Ceramics and Glass Section of the Department of Conservation, officially declared the Vase to be in an unstable condition, and undertook to attempt a third restoration. The Vase was booked to take a leading role in a temporary exhibition, 'Glass of the Caesars'. After this, it would be starring in the new Roman Gallery, but between the two it might take a sabbatical of a few months, while the work was carried out.

Williams's first task was to investigate the techniques of his predecessors. He found little on Doubleday, but after so long this was no surprise. He was more taken aback by a complete lack of documentation for Axtell's work, as the man had still been employed by the museum when Williams joined the staff in 1961. Williams wanted to know what kind of adhesive Axtell had used, because he was going to have to remove it in order to reduce the Vase to its constituent parts before building it up again. Unable to find any written records, Williams was reduced to canvassing his colleagues for their recollections, and the results were conflicting: epoxy resin, shellac, animal glue, or a mixture of these were all confidently put forward by different individuals.

To begin the process of dissolution the Vase was wrapped in blotting paper overlaid with dental plaster, inside and out, further reinforced by flexible plastic clamps. Thus mummified, the Vase was then placed in a bowl of water. Solvents were added, and after three days one of the handles was gingerly prodded; it moved. The Vase was taken out of its softening bath, and gradually the plaster-lined paper was peeled off, starting at the rim. As the paper was pulled away, the fragments could be picked off one by one. After a day's painstaking disassembly, during which each piece was numbered and its position on the Vase recorded, the Vase was in pieces, and Williams found 189 fragments. Each one was put under the microscope, so that the remains of the adhesive (which turned out to be an early epoxy resin) could be scraped off with a surgical scalpel, and then washed in warm water. The Vase clearly needed a wash; it was very dirty, and the pieces came out of their bath markedly improved in appearance. The cleaning process allowed the conservators to begin to familiarise themselves with the individual pieces and plan how they would be put together again.

The fragments were all laid out, reproducing Doubleday's watercolour jigsaw, and Williams and his team confronted the most daunting aspect of their task; Williams had already carried out the restoration of the celebrated Sutton Hoo helmet, and confessed that he well knew how terrifying it was to have a world-famous object in bits while doubts as to whether he would ever be able to put it together again began to seep in. To make matters worse a camera crew stood at his shoulder, recording every move for a BBC television documentary. Williams not only had to suffer this extra scrutiny, but also felt under pressure to complete his work in order to fit in with the documentary-maker's deadline.

As expected, sticking the Vase back together proved more difficult than pulling it apart. The most long-lasting, powerful and up-to-date epoxy glue had been chosen, but it took days to dry, and as it did so fragments carefully put together would slide out of place. The answer to this was a complicated process whereby a secondary, faster adhesive would be used on one small section of one of the surfaces being stuck together. This would hold the pieces together until the stronger glue took effect. This faster-acting glue, a sort of superglue, dried in seconds when subjected to ultraviolet light. So the technique was perfected, and the process of reconstruction could begin.

This had to be planned carefully; there is a risk when fitting together fragments that if the pieces are stuck together in the wrong order, subsequent pieces will not be left room to fit in snugly. This problem is called a 'trap out' in the restoring business, and in order to avoid it, construction of a fragmented vessel like the Vase is usually begun from a large piece, or a base piece, to which other pieces can then be added. Two areas of the Vase were made up of fragments with obvious, close-fitting joins, which could be easily built into large sections. These then provided the starting point, and gradually the Vase began to grow around these foundations. The real trouble lay around the neck and shoulder of the Vase, which had taken the force of Mulcahy's blow, and were the most badly shattered. No satisfactory alignment could at first be found for the myriad tiny slivers in this section. The upper part of the Vase was assembled, taken apart, and reassembled as various configurations were tried and rejected for several frustrating weeks until finally a solution was found, and the last piece fitted into the rim of the Vase. The Vase was now left for three weeks to allow the adhesive to harden and set.

There were still small holes in the Vase, places where the original glass was entirely missing, and these needed to be filled. The first step was to create a backing to these holes; strips of wax were laid across the inside of the Vase, and then a coloured resin was brushed into the holes, slowly built up to just above the surface of the Vase, and the excess then wiped away. Once hardened, this resin was polished and shaped, until it closely resembled the glass around it, without being completely undetectable, so that the attentive visitor can still see what is original and what has been added. The entire process took nine months; then the Vase went back on show, taking pride of place in the new gallery.

While the restorers refurbished the Vase, its reputation was similarly enhanced by the work of scholars concerning themselves with its dating and provenance. Gradually, the emphasis shifted; as academics studied the political iconography of the Augustan period, they began to realise that the figures on the Vase might not simply depict a well-worn story from mythology, but might rather have a much closer relationship with whoever commissioned it. Over the last few decades of the twentieth century an entirely new theory began to emerge, which gives the Vase a place of the highest honour in the Roman world: a direct association with the Emperor Augustus himself.

Eighteenth Fragment
The Emperor Augustus

Recent theories about the figures on the Vase have tended more and more towards an explanation related to the politics of late Republican Rome and the early Augustan period. German academic Erica Simon took a long hard look at the Vase in the 1950s, and came up with a new theory, supported by a passage in the Roman historian Suetonius's *The Twelve Caesars*, which contains his account of the life of the Emperor Augustus. At the end of this account Suetonius discusses, in his wonderfully gossipy style, portents and omens that were said to have accompanied the birth of the future Emperor, including one he found in a book 'called *Theologumena*, by Asclepias of Mendes'. It is, in essence, the story of a divine rape:

Augustus's mother, Atia, upon attending at midnight a solemn religious ceremony at the temple of Apollo, when the rest of the married women retired, fell asleep on her couch in the temple. A serpent crept up to her, entered her, and then glided away. Awakening, she purified herself, as usual after the embraces of her husband. Instantly there appeared upon her body a mark in the form of a serpent, which made her ashamed to visit the public baths. Augustus was born nine months later, and for that reason was thought to be the son of Apollo.

This story provided Simon with the key to her fresh interpretation. She decided that both sides of the Vase refer to this myth: Figure A is Apollo, Figure C is Atia, with Apollo in the form of a serpent popping up between her legs, before or after the act of impregnation, and figure D is Chronos, prophet of the good times to come under the rule of Augustus, the result of this union. On the second side, Figure E is Apollo again, Figure F is Atia once more – falling asleep at the temple, perhaps – and Figure G is Venus, presiding over their fruitful encounter. Simon quoted several images of a sleeping woman with her arm raised to her head, being approached by a snake, which are found in artworks of the time of Augustus's reign, and are associated with his birth and considered to be works of propaganda for his cause. The masks beneath the handles represent Capricorn, the constellation under which Augustus was born, as Suetonius again mentions in another story concerning portents of Augustus's greatness. The historian tells how Augustus reluctantly accompanied his friend Agrippa to visit an astrologer called Theogenes. Agrippa got such a glowing prophecy that Augustus hung back, not willing to let himself in for something he assumed would be rather less exciting:

Being persuaded, however, after much importunity, he declared it. Theogenes started up from his seat, and abased himself to Augustus. Not long afterwards, now confident of the greatness of his destiny, Augustus published his horoscope, and struck a silver coin, bearing upon it the sign of Capricorn, under the influence of which he was born.

Simon's theory was also prompted by the efforts of modern scholars to date the Vase; their findings, as we will see, put the likely date of the Vase's creation as sometime during the reign of Augustus, and Simon's overall conclusion is that the Vase was a piece of propaganda in Augustus's campaign to legitimise the power he had seized during the last, bloody struggles of the Civil War.

Augustus was first of the Roman emperors. His given name was Octavius – 'Augustus' was a title conferred later. Octavius was born into the merchant class, but his mother was a niece of Julius Caesar, and seventeen-year-old Octavius was given a post on the staff of the Emperor, who was then campaigning in Spain. Julius Caesar liked and admired his nephew, and made him his heir. When Julius Caesar was murdered this gave young Octavius a political opportunity, of which he made the most. He set himself up as an equal and rival to Mark Antony, who was Caesar's right-hand man and political successor. Together they hunted down and killed Julius's assassins and other enemies of the Julian faction; after decades of civil war, these were many. A reign of terror was instituted, known as the proscriptions, during which lists of thousands of political opponents were compiled, for summary execution. Still only nineteen years old, Octavius seized control of several Roman legions, and marched on Rome itself. Then Octavius and Mark Antony agreed to divide the Roman world between them. But a propaganda war was already being fought between the two, during which, for instance, Mark Antony accused Octavius of submitting to his uncle's sexual advances. Even the marriage of Mark Antony to Octavius's sister could not prevent the inevitable clash, and when Mark Antony abandoned his wife for the charms of Cleopatra, Octavius was provided with his pretext for war. The two opposing forces fought a decisive sea battle at Actium, and Mark Antony was defeated by Octavius's lieutenant Agrippa. (Octavius, no general himself, had a habit of falling sick before battles.) At the age of thirty-three, Octavius had made himself absolute ruler of the known world, and the Senate hailed him as Caesar Augustus.

Augustus was faced with a problem: his uncle Julius had been assassinated because he had too openly flirted with the role of absolute monarch. Augustus needed to sell himself as a man who respected the Republican virtues and tradition. In the Senate he pretended to give up his power. 'I am mild by nature,' he said, 'and have no wish to dominate. Allow me to live out my life in peace.'

Officially Augustus resigned from almost all offices; he wanted to create an illusion of a return to constitutional government. He would be just a humble administrator, albeit a rather successful one. He initiated building projects on a massive scale. According to the Roman historian Strabo, 'the Romans and their allies ... never enjoyed such peace and prosperity as that provided by Caesar Augustus.' He was just the hard-working, pious, modest, clean-living servant of the people, and at best merely the 'first among equals'.

This policy was accompanied by a propaganda campaign orchestrated by Augustus's friend Maecenas. Maecenas had at his command a significant sample of the greatest writers in Roman literature: the poets Horace, Virgil and Propertius. All eagerly embraced the myth, either out of political necessity or because they genuinely welcomed it after so much bloodshed. (The poet Ovid, who did not toe the line quite so assiduously, found himself banished to the Black Sea, the ends of the earth so far as he was concerned, and spent the rest of his life writing abject letters to the Emperor begging to be allowed to return home.) Horace wrote effusive odes in praise of Augustus and Agrippa. Virgil prophesied a 'golden age', presided over by the benign and godlike Augustus, and penned his epic *Aeneid,* in which the Trojan prince Aeneas flees the ruins of Troy to found the city of Rome.

Augustus carefully cultivated the image of a simple man; he lived frugally, sleeping in the same simply furnished room, wearing fine clothes only on state occasions, eating plain food and even advocating plain speech. He championed a return to the 'traditional values' of the Republic; morality laws were passed, and louche behaviour punished by the state. An example was made of an actor called Pylades. When a member of the audience hissed his performance, Pylades responded with 'an obscene movement of his middle finger', and for this he was banished from Italy. But this was all a show; Augustus was careful to accumulate and keep all real power, in particular the command of the legions, and he controlled the vast financial resources of the Empire. As for the pious chastity of the Republic, Augustus was sexually voracious, with a predilection for deflowering virgins. He was a serial adulterer who defended his actions to his friends by explaining that he slept with the wives and daughters of his enemies in order to discover their plans. His daughter Julia ran out of control in wild promiscuity, laying the basis for the subsequent reputation of the Roman orgy, and even, according to Suetonius, living out a courtesan-fantasy by selling her body to the highest bidder.

In his youth, before he decided that in order to wield power he must dispense with its trappings, Augustus had felt the urge to collect. He liked curiosities of all sorts, amassed a collection of ancient weapons and skeletons and had a particular weakness for vases. During the proscriptions graffiti appeared on the base of his statue referring to this, as well as to his father's mercantile background:

> I do not take my father's line;
> His trade was silver coin, but mine
> Corinthian vases.

There was a rumour that he added names of men to the list of those to be killed because they owned vases that he coveted and could subsequently confiscate for his collection. After he defeated Mark Antony and marched into Alexandria to ransack the palace of Queen Cleopatra, he kept nothing for himself – the policy of public self-denial was already in operation – except for a 'murrhine', or glass vase.

*

The theory that the figures relate directly to Augustus's myth is underpinned by the dating of the Vase, and its attribution: recent research has revealed not only a possible date for the creation of the Vase, but even a tentative identification of the craftsman who carved it. In an article written at the end of the 1980s, Kenneth Painter and David Whitehouse elaborated on Simon's interpretation of the figures on the Vase and took it one step further. Figure C was certainly Atia, the mother of Augustus, and figure D was Neptune, the god of the sea, by whose favour the battle of Actium was won and Augustus's rule begun. The date of the battle was also, by pure coincidence, Augustus's birthday, and thus the most significant in his myth. According to Whitehouse and Painter, Side II shows the birth of Paris. In the myth, Paris's mother Hecuba, Queen of Troy, dreams that she gives birth to a burning torch which sets light to the whole city, a portent of the havoc her son will cause. This is why the child is exposed to die on a hillside, but he is rescued by shepherds, with whom he then lives and among whom Jupiter spots him when he is looking around for some unsuspecting mortal to decide which of the three goddesses Juno, Minerva and Venus is the fairest.

So figure F is Hecuba, E is Paris himself, and G is Venus, to whom Paris gives the prize and who rewards him with mortal Helen, thus precipitating the Trojan War and neatly fulfilling the prophecy. The

[218]

rocks on which Hecuba lies, as she clutches the ill-omened torch of her dream, represent the ruins of Troy, as does the fallen capital at her feet. So the two sides of the Vase show the ruin of Troy, and the birth of a new, Augustan Rome. Figure A, claim Whitehouse and Painter, seeing a resemblance between this and other depictions of the Emperor, is none other than Augustus himself.

Whitehouse and Painter draw attention to another resemblance, between the workmanship on the Vase and that of an engraved gem in the collection of the Duke of Devonshire. This gemstone, a carnelian less than two centimetres high, is carved with the figure of the Greek warrior Diomedes. The face, hair, musculature and pose of this figure are all strikingly similar to those of figure A on the Vase, so much so that one could assume that they were both carved by the same hand. The obvious conclusion is that the gem and the Vase were both the work of a single craftsman. But unlike the Vase, the gem is signed, in Greek letters, with the name Dioskourides. The fame of Dioskourides has lasted. He is known to have carved portraits of Julius Caesar, and one of Augustus himself. Did he also, therefore, carve the Vase? Did he carve it for his imperial patron?

Augustus enjoyed – insisted on – propaganda to further his cause. He had a predilection for glass vases, and the resources to commission the finest work that craftsmen could produce. It is conceivable, therefore, that the Portland Vase was made for his personal pleasure, to celebrate the myth of his divine origins. It is possible that the Portland Vase belonged to the Emperor Augustus himself.

Nineteenth Fragment

Posterity

It might appear that, barring accidents, the story of the Vase is over. It sits comfortably in its case in the Gallery of Roman Antiquities, secure in the knowledge that its fame will ensure it a permanent place among the highlights of the collection. The British Museum has given the Vase a home for nearly two centuries, and has owned it outright for sixty years. It will not now part with one of its most celebrated treasures, and unless the Vase is the victim of another accident, or another deranged attack, or 'enemy action', the most it can expect is to be carefully taken apart and put back together again in another hundred years or so, when the current restoration has aged, and another generation of restorers begin to look at the records of their predecessors to discover what adhesive was used way back in the twentieth century. Presumably, the Vase will stay in the Museum until civilisation, or London, or both, come to an end – or perhaps just democracy and its institutions will be overthrown, and as Fate inexorably turns her wheel the Vase, looted from the galleries, will once again end up in the private collection of some despot or billionaire.

But even in the foreseeable future the story is not over: far from it, because the controversy over the significance of the figures on the Vase continues to rage unabated, hotter than ever, and will very possibly never come to any satisfactory conclusion. The stakes have never been higher. As recently as 2003 an American academic, Jerome M. Eisenberg, made a startling announcement based upon his reading of the figures, and once again the *Times* devoted headlines to the Vase. Eisenberg's theory was subsequently published in the reputable international journal *Minerva*, devoted to art and archaeology, of which Eisenberg himself is editor-in-chief.

Eisenberg based his theory on several points: first, the mystery surrounding the discovery of the Vase, which throws doubt on its provenance; secondly, the multiplicity of theories regarding the interpretation of the figures, which suggests to Eisenberg that it is not the academics who are to blame for failing to come up with a convincing theory, but the fault of the Vase itself for neglecting to display a coherent theme. Finally, Eisenberg detects what he describes as 'numerous stylistic inconsistencies' between the Vase and 'genuine' ancient artefacts. Eisenberg maintains that the reason the figures on the Vase cannot be identified is that they were made not in Ancient Rome, but during the Renaissance, when a sixteenth-century artist carved the figures by copying them from various ancient works, but without himself understanding what these figures might be. This artist, whoever he was, did not have a proper understanding of classical mythology, and recklessly strewed his figures around the Vase, heedless of the fact that he would be giving scholars headaches for centuries to come. According to Eisenberg, this unknown sixteenth-century craftsman adapted and misinterpreted figures from various pre-existing marble sculptures carved in relief, in particular from a Roman sarcophagus of the third century AD, which displays a scene in which Mars, god of war, approaches Rhea Silvia, the princess who, as a result of their union, gives birth to Romulus and Remus, the founders of Rome. The figure of Rhea on this sarcophagus does bear some resemblance to figure F on the Vase; she reclines, one hand raised to her head, the lower half of her body covered in drapery.

Eisenberg also finds sources for the other figures on the Vase, and other inconsistencies. Nowhere in ancient art can he find a representation of Cupid within a group in which the winged god is actually in flight. Roman goddesses were usually depicted wearing sandals; the feet of all three female figures on the Vase, human or divine, are bare. No male figure is depicted dropping a garment in ancient art – as Figure A does – except on the Vase. The serpent with Figure C is a mixture of various different creatures, cobbled together by the Renaissance artist. The very quality of the carving undermines its ancient provenance; Eisenberg suggests that only with the Renaissance did artistic talents great enough to carve such figures arise.

Eisenberg's conclusion is that the Vase was manufactured by one of the talented cameo engravers working in Rome in the sixteenth century, and produced in order to satisfy a demand for works of ancient art. He speculates that because the most powerful Roman families at that time – the Medici, Borghese, Farnese and Ludovisi – had a virtual monopoly on ancient sculpture, the Vase was commissioned by Fabrizio Lazzaro or Cardinal Francesco del Monte, so that the latter could 'upstage' the others.

Eisenberg's theory is certainly ingenious, addressing as it does the twin mysteries of the Vase's origins and its figures. How can the Vase be dated scientifically? Glass cannot be subject to carbon dating, a technique that can only be used on organic matter, animal or vegetable. The glass of the Vase has been analysed; an opportunity to subject it to laboratory testing was created by Mr Crocker of Putney, who brought the little box of glass chips back to the Museum in the 1940s, forgotten since Doubleday's restoration a century before. The Research Laboratory of the British Museum has examined these chips using various methods. They have been put under the electron microscope, and surveyed by 'non-destructive qualitative X-ray fluorescence spectroscopy'. Interesting findings have come to light: the proportions of the ingredients of the glass – soda, lime and silica – have been shown to resemble those of other Ancient Roman glassware, but these results are in no way conclusive. The only way the Vase can be dated is by comparing it with other objects: in other words, by interpretation. Why should not Eisenberg's comparison with the work of Renaissance artists be as valid as any with older works? In order to test his theory it is necessary to examine other examples of Roman cameo glass.

Roman cameo glass vessels are rare; just over a dozen pieces exist in any state of preservation. Given the fragile nature of the medium perhaps this is not surprising. More telling is the rarity of even fragments of cameo glass; there are fewer than two hundred of these. Considering the scale and wealth of Rome, and the fairly persistent activities of archaeologists and treasure-hunters over the centuries, this is a startlingly small quantity. Of the few surviving pieces two in particular bear comparison with the Portland Vase. Both are cameo works, in blue and white. Both, crucially, were discovered during the excavations in Pompeii. This means that they themselves can be confidently dated to ancient times, and to a period no later than the date of the eruption that engulfed Pompeii in AD 79.

One of these objects is a jug, known as the Auldjo Jug, and it too is in the possession of the British Museum. It is not complete, nor is the carving on it as elaborate as that on the Portland Vase, but there are very strong similarities. The Auldjo Jug is decorated with a design of vine leaves, ivy and laurel, in which perch small birds. The style of the carving is so similar to the Portland Vase's that it has been suggested that they are both products of the same workshop. The other object is known as the Blue Vase. The Blue Vase is also a cameo work in blue and white glass. It is decorated even more elaborately than the Portland Vase, with great swirls of vines, and a gang of cupids harvesting the grapes, treading them, playing musical instruments and generally having a gay old time. Beside the Portland Vase, this decoration looks very busy and decadent. But there is one striking point of similarity. At the base of one of the scenes on the Blue Vase, right in the centre, is a square object like a fallen capital, with a notch cut in it, on which rests the foot of one of the cupids. It is exactly the same as the object depicted on the Portland Vase under the foot of figure F. It is the same shape, in the same position: at the bottom of the scene, in the middle. It has been suggested that this object is some kind of signature, indicating that both the Portland Vase and the Blue Vase came from the same workshop.

The Blue Vase was found in Pompeii in the 1830s; its discovery was recorded because it took place during a royal visit. On 29 December 1837, Ferdinand II, King of the Two Sicilies, was inspecting the excavations, and a tomb belonging to the House of the Mosaics was opened in his presence. Inside this tomb was the Blue Vase, still containing the ashes with which it had been interred. In fact, we cannot take this discovery at face value; it was the practice of the excavators to open a tomb, then close it up, and re-excavate it for the benefit of watching VIPs, in order to avoid any embarrassing anticlimaxes. It is even possible that the Blue Vase was found elsewhere in the excavation, filled with ashes and planted in the tomb in order to impress the King. But it is beyond dispute that the Blue Vase was discovered at Pompeii, and therefore must have been made earlier than AD 79. It is thus not possible that any Renaissance artist,

[225]

living and working three centuries or so before the discovery of the Blue Vase, would have been aware of the images on it. Yet Eisenberg suggests that it was such an artist who created the scene on the Portland Vase, complete with its trademark fallen capital. The coincidence is too great. Despite its stylistic differences, the Blue Vase anchors the Portland Vase firmly in the ancient era, and Eisenberg's theory, however beguiling, cannot hold: the Vase is not a fake.

Moreover, a spirited reply to his accusation was promptly forthcoming from the British Museum itself. Susan Walker, Deputy Keeper of Greek and Roman Antiquities, respectfully pointed out the strong resemblance between the iconography on the Vase and that of other cameo vessels of the Roman period. She also took the opportunity to present her own entirely original and highly persuasive theory about the figures, relating them to the politics surrounding the rise of Augustus, and once again seeing the Vase as a work of pro-Augustan propaganda.

Walker begins with Side I, which she considers to be a seduction scene: Figure C reaches out to Figure A in a gesture that will precipitate an erotic embrace. She points out that this seduction is taking place outdoors, and that this is very unusual in Roman art of the period. Sex – which is quite often depicted on Roman glass and silverware, as well as in the notorious wall-paintings of Pompeii – always takes place indoors. The outdoor setting is therefore significant: it implies something particularly abandoned about the behaviour of the figures here. Figure C, then, is a female seducer, and of the short-list of famous seductresses of myth and history, Walker selects the most notorious: Cleopatra. She suggests that Figure C – Cleopatra, together with her 'serpent of old Nile' – is reaching out to Mark Antony, whom she famously bedded during the closing stages of the Civil War. Figure D is the son of Hercules, the mythical hero with whom Antony identified; he looks on disapprovingly at the unheroic self-indulgence to which Antony has abandoned himself.

The swooning lady on Side II, Figure F, is none other than Octavia, Augustus's sister. When Antony and Augustus divided the empire between them, Octavia was given to Antony in marriage in order to cement this alliance. Cleopatra's superior charms did serious damage to the marriage, but in an attempt to heal the rift, Octavia, who had been left in Rome while Antony sported in Egypt, travelled out to meet her husband with men and money for his eastern campaigns. He took the reinforcements and packed her back off to Rome, thus providing Augustus, her outraged brother, with a pretext for war and the final showdown between the two which culminated at the battle of Actium. Figure E is Augustus, about to rise and revenge his abandoned sister, while Figure G is Venus, who presided over the fortunes of Augustus, and is now reassuring him that he will emerge the victor. According to this theory the Vase was therefore commissioned by, if not the Emperor himself, then someone close to his cause, after the victory at Actium, in order to commemorate the struggles which Augustus had successfully overcome, and this dark moment in the fortunes of his family.

It is quite remarkable, and a testimony to both Susan Walker's learning and the endless fascination of the Vase, that even now, after so many have been proposed, a fresh, entirely new and perfectly plausible theory can be concocted. The game, it would seem, can be played indefinitely. Whatever the relative merits of any interpretation, the truth is that there can be no final, definitive solution, because the necessary knowledge is lost to us, and perhaps Bernard Ashmole came closest to the mystery when he suggested this. There are not enough clear attributes given to the figures on the Vase to allow us to identify them with any certainty. There are, however, just enough clues to tempt us to try, and try we have, and will; it is in our nature. In this respect the story of the Vase can have no ending, until the limits of human ingenuity are reached, and human ingenuity may well prove to be infinite.

*

Imagine the many figures who have possessed the Vase all standing in some kind of timeline down the Greek and Roman Galleries of the British Museum. At the beginning of the queue, away down the far end of the gallery, is an anonymous Roman glass-blower, horny-handed in his leather smock. Next to him stands the diatretarius or engraver, perhaps Dioskourides himself; then Augustus Caesar, in his simple robe, small in stature but giving off the charisma of power like radioactivity. A shadowy parade of later Caesars continues the line, ending – if the story of the finding of the Vase has any truth – with Alexander Severus, the well-meaning but doomed young paragon.

At this point in the line there is an abrupt change; the next figure has exchanged Roman robes for sixteenth-century britches and stockings. He is Fabrizio Lazzaro, holding his lantern and his shovel, and after him comes Cardinal del Monte, in his robes and affability, and Maffeo Barberini, wearing the papal tiara and flanked by his nephews. Several generations of Barberini follow, gradually less sumptuously dressed, until we reach the cash-strapped figure of Donna Cornelia Barberini-Colonna, Princess of Palestrina. Here the line changes again: Italian faces give way to Northern ones; the dry and vinegary aspect of James Byres; tall, beaky Sir William Hamilton, with the Star of the Garter on his chest, young and lovely Emma on his arm, and an ironical gleam in his eye. After him, the dumpy figure of the Duchess of Portland, swaddled in her seven cloaks, and accompanied by her bonneted and scissor-wielding companion. Then comes the line of Dukes: the Third, frowning with the demands of office; the Fourth, hale and hearty in his riding-boots; the Fifth, in his

ancholy; the Sixth, peering into
…er whom there are no owners of
…n of the Keepers of the British
…dy and pipe-smoking, then
…you and me. Other figures stand
…it: John Doubleday with his
…iam Blake with their engraving
…sper copy; Cassiano dal Pozzo
…m; Tommaso Campanella in his
…r behind a display case, the
…clutching his lump of basalt.
…principles of the Museum, the
…and stand by the case in which
…end of this line, as part-owner
…– of all previous owners. The
…nd participant in the last two
…f the whole human family. It
…t still the same, flawed and
…vhat mysterious. Perhaps, in
…ome, and put some flowers in

JASCHIN — (56) 270

Death in Venice
T. Mann (1875 – 1955)

Janek Fradowski.

(see TADZIO)
+ G. Mahler – 1860 – 1911

Bibliography

Ackroyd, P., *Blake: a biography* (Ballantine, 1995).

Anson, E. and F. Anson, eds, *Mary Hamilton, afterwards Mrs John Dickenson, at court and at home. From letters and diaries, 1756 to 1816* (John Murray, 1925).

Ashmole, B., 'A New Interpretation of the Portland Vase' *Journal of Hellenic Studies* 87 (1967).

Beard, G. W., *Nineteenth-Century Cameo Glass* (Ceramic Book Company, 1956).

Bimson, M., and I. C. Freestone, 'An analytical study of the relationship between the Portland Vase and Other Roman Glass Cameos' *Journal of Glass Studies* 25 (1983).

Black, J., *The Grand Tour* (Sutton, 1992).

Blunt, A., *Nicolas Poussin* (Bollingen Foundation, 1967).

Brown, E. L., 'The Portland Vase' *American Journal of Archaeology* 74 (1970).

Castiglione, B., *The Book of the Courtier*. Trans. Hoby (Dent, 1974).

Caygill, M., 'Whodunit?' *British Museum Society Bulletin* 48 (1985).

—,*Treasures of the British Museum* (British Museum, 1985).

Caygill, M., and C. Date, *Building the British Museum* (British Museum, 1999).

Clairmont, C. W., 'A Note on the Portland Vase' *American Journal of Archaeology* 72 (1968).

Clarke, M., and P. Nicholas, *The Arrogant Connoisseur: Richard Payne Knight, 1751-1824* (Manchester University Press, 1983).

[231]

Constantine, D., *Fields of Fire: a life of Sir William Hamilton* (Phoenix, 2001).

Eisenberg, Jerome M., 'The Portland Vase: further observations' *Minerva* 14 (August 2003).

Farrer, K. E., ed., *Correspondence of Josiah Wedgwood 1781-94* (London, 1903).

Fothergill, B., *Sir William Hamilton, Envoy Extraordinary* (Faber and Faber, 1969).

—, *The Strawberry Hill Set: Horace Walpole and his circle* (Faber and Faber, 1983).

Gibbon, E., *The Decline and Fall of the Roman Empire* (1776-87, repr. Everyman, 1993).

—, *Memoirs of Edward Gibbon, written by himself, and a selection from his letters, with notes by John, Lord Sheffield.* Ed. H. Morley (Routledge, 1891).

Goethe, J. W., *Travels in Italy, together with his Second Residence in Rome and Fragments on Italy.* Trans. Morrison and Nisbet (G. Bell and Sons, 1892).

Grabsky, P., *I, Caesar: ruling the Roman Empire* (BBC, 1997).

Gray, J. M., *James and William Tassie* (Edinburgh, 1894).

Harden, D. B., *Glass of the Caesars* (Olivetti, 1987).

—, *Masterpieces of Glass: a selection* (British Museum, 1968).

Harrison, E. B., 'The Portland Vase: Thinking it Over' *Essays in Archaeology and the Humanities.* Ed. L. Bonfante and H. von Heintze (von Zabern Verlag, 1976).

Haskell, F., *Patrons and Painters: a study in the relations between Italian art and society in the age of the Baroque* (Yale University Press, 1980).

Haynes, D. E. L., *The Portland Vase* (British Museum, 1975).

Hibbert, C., *The Grand Tour* (Spring Books, 1974).

Hind, J. G. F., 'Greek and Roman Epic Scenes on the Portland Vase' *Journal of Hellenic Studies* 99 (1979).

Ingamells, J., *A Dictionary of British and Irish Travellers in Italy* (Yale University Press, 1997).

Jenkins, I. D., ed., *Vases and Volcanoes* (British Museum, 1996).

Karslake, B., 'Early Days of the Portland Vase' *Country Life* 171 (1982).

Lewis, S., ed. *Catalogue to the Sale of the Duchess of Portland's Museum* (Grolier, n.d.).

Llanover, Lady A., ed., *The Autobiography and Correspondence of Mary*

Granville, Mrs Delany: with interesting reminiscences of King George the Third and Queen Charlotte (R. Bentley, 1862).

Langdon, H., *Caravaggio: a life* (Chatto and Windus, 1998).

Leppman, W., *Winckelmann* (Victor Gollancz, 1971).

Magnusson, T., *Rome in the Age of Bernini* (Humanities Press, 1982).

Mankowitz, W., *The Portland Vase and the Wedgwood Copies* (Deutsch, 1952).

Miller, E., *That Noble Cabinet: a history of the British Museum* (Deutsch, 1973).

Moore, Dr J., *A View of Society and Manners in Italy* (London, 1790).

Mowl, T., *Horace Walpole: the great outsider* (John Murray, 1996).

Neuburg, F., *Ancient Glass*. Trans. Bullock and Jaffa (Barrie and Rockliff, 1962).

Newby, M., ed., *Early Imperial Roman Glass* (London, 1990).

— and K. Painter, eds, *Roman Glass: two centuries of art and invention* (Society of Antiquaries of London, 1991).

Nicolson, Sir H. G., *The Age of Reason: 1770-1789* (Constable, 1960).

Northwood, J., 'Noteworthy Productions of the Glass Craftsman's Art. I. The Reproduction of the Portland Vase' *Journal of the Society of Glass Technology* 8 (1924).

Painter, K., and D. Whitehouse, 'Recent Research on the Portland Vase' *Journal of Glass Studies* 32 (1990).

Pastor, L. von, *The History of the Popes from the Close of the Middle Ages: drawn from the secret archives of the Vatican and other original sources*. Ed. and trans. Antrobus and Kerr (Routledge and Kegan Paul, 1902).

Portland, W., Duke of, *Men, Women and Things: memories of the Duke of Portland* (Faber and Faber, 1937).

Ranke, L. von, *The Ecclesiastical and Political History of the Popes of Rome During the Sixteenth and Seventeenth Centuries*. Trans. Austin (London 1868).

Raspe, R. E., *A Descriptive Catalogue of a General Collection of Ancient and Modern Engraved Gems, cameos as well as intaglios* (J. Tassie and J. Murray, 1791).

Reilly, R., *Josiah Wedgwood, 1730-1795* (Macmillan, 1992).

—, *Wedgwood: the new illustrated dictionary* (Antique Collector's Club, 1995).

Reston, J., *Galileo: a life* (Cassell, 1994).

Schnapp, A., *The Discovery of the Past: the origins of archaeology* (British Museum, 1996).

Scott, J. B., *Images of Nepotism: the painted ceilings of Palazzo Barberini* (Princeton University Press, 1991).

Smart, J. D., 'The Portland Vase Again' *Journal of Hellenic Studies* 104 (1984).

Stuart-Jones, H., 'The British School at Rome' *The Athenaeum* 4244 (1909).

Suetonius, *The Lives of the Twelve Caesars*. Trans. Thomson (G. Bell and Sons, 1903).

Tassie, J., *A Catalogue of Impressions in Sulphur of antique and modern gems from which pastes are made and sold* (London, 1775).

Trethewey, R., *Mistress of the Arts* (Review, 2002).

Turberville, A. S., *A History of Welbeck Abbey and its Owners* (Faber and Faber, 1939).

Vermuele, C., *European Art and the Classical Past* (Harvard University Press, 1964).

Vose, R. H., *Glass* (Ebury, 1975).

Walker, D. P., *Spiritual and Demonic Magic: from Ficino to Campanella* (Notre Dame University Press, 1975).

Wedgwood, J., *Reprint of a Description of the Portland Vase with notes by T. Windus* (London, 1845).

Williams, N., *The Breaking and Remaking of the Portland Vase* (British Museum, 1989).

Wilson, M., *The Life of William Blake* (Oxford University Press, 1971).

Windus, T., *A New Elucidation of the Subjects on the Celebrated Portland Vase, formerly called the Barberini: and the sarcophagus in which it was discovered* (London, 1845).

Zanker, P., *The Power of Images in the Age of Augustus*. Trans. Shapiro (University of Michigan Press, 1988).

Index